Freedom's Voice

G·K
Hall
&Co.

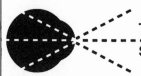 This Large Print Book carries the
Seal of Approval of N.A.V.H.

Freedom's Voice

The Perilous Present and Uncertain Future of the First Amendment

Robert D. Richards

G.K. Hall & Co. • Thorndike, Maine

Published in 2000 by arrangement with Batsford Brassey, Inc.

G.K. Hall Large Print American History Series.

The text of this Large Print edition is unabridged.
Other aspects of the book may vary from the original edition.

Set in 16 pt. Plantin by Warren S. Doersam.

Printed in the United States on permanent paper.

Library of Congress Cataloging-in-Publication Data

Richards, Robert D., 1962–
   Freedom's voice : the perilous present and uncertain future of the
first amendment / Robert D. Richards.
     p. cm.
   Originally published: Washington, D.C. : Brassey's, c1998.
   Includes bibliographical references.
   ISBN 0-7838-8978-X (lg. print : hc : alk. paper)
   1. Freedom of speech — United States. I. Title.
KF4772.R53 2000
342.73′0853—dc21   99-087988

To
Anne Elizabeth and Matthew Ryan

Contents

Preface

When James Madison crafted the simple but powerful words that became the First Amendment to the United States Constitution, he could not in all likelihood have envisioned the turbulent and vibrant path his words would take — but perhaps he had some idea. Ironically, Madison was, at first, against any amendments to the Constitution, believing they would weaken the document, if not the government itself. Over time, he came to recognize the political expediency of the Bill of Rights. The founders of this nation created a living document, one that would grow and mature with the ages and be shaped and strengthened by life's circumstances. Yet, growing pains, although difficult, are usually associated with a general feeling that growth is a good thing. Unfortunately, this underlying commonality has begun to disintegrate. Some surveys even show that a majority of Americans would vote against the First Amendment if it were placed on a national referendum today.

Although it has weathered more than two centuries of constant use and prevailed during periods of war and cold war, upheaval and uncertainty, the First Amendment remains a national enigma. The public has grown weary of seeing the First Amendment dragged out as the savior of the unsavory set, such as those who traffic in pornography or focus their cameras on human tragedy. Much too often the depth of the public's understanding of free speech principles stops there. People are too quick and too willing to judge the First Amendment solely by the company it keeps, but doing so misses the extraordinary reach of First Amendment jurisprudence. It also masks the immense contribution to democratic self-governance that is embodied in this premier constitutional principle.

This book was written as an argument in favor of paying greater attention to the health of the First Amendment. The topics chosen purposely range from the little known to the famous. Some of the subjects are the ones that people talk about in the bars, hair salons, restaurants, and neighborhood hangouts of America. Others are debated in classrooms and boardrooms and community meeting halls throughout the country. Some topics have generated enormous media attention while others scarcely get a mention. Still, all the issues discussed in this book deserve attention; moreover, they build the case for safeguarding the freedoms so many have fought to create and strengthen.

This First Amendment story is told primarily through people — the beneficiaries of constitutional protections, the victims of egregious violations of free speech and press, and other key players in this vital constitutional match. The law is presented in a deliberately unassuming manner so as to not make the reader lose sight of the grassroots nature of constitutional doctrine. After all, the Bill of Rights was not written for the amusement of scholars in a think tank. It was written as a guarantee of liberty for the citizenry of the United States. The goal of this book is to open up avenues of discussion and contribute to a renaissance of enthusiastic vigilance for sharpening the key tool in participatory democracy.

I would like to thank the dozens of people who were willing to sit down and talk with me about the First Amendment. Their thoughts, ideas, and quotes fill the pages of this book. My students deserve a word of thanks as well. As I teach about the First Amendment, they help to check and clarify my own thinking about the subject and foreshadow what the next generation of leaders will bring to the democracy. The Freedom Forum, through a Professors Publishing Program grant, made it possible for me to travel across the country and talk to the people who help to shape or are shaped by the First Amendment, and I am forever grateful. The Freedom Forum has contributed enormously to the preservation of "Free Press, Free Speech, and Free Spirit." I would also like to thank my colleagues in Pennsylvania State University's College of Communications who encourage this First Amendment zealot despite occasional untoward consequences, especially Clay Calvert, a dedicated First Amendment scholar who works tirelessly with me on many projects. I thank Heidi Hendershott, Ray Niekamp, and Kati Razzano for their valuable research assistance. I am also grateful to Betsy Hall for her invaluable computer assistance in preparing the manuscript. Special thanks goes as well to CNN's senior Washington correspondent, Charles Bierbauer, for his help in setting up interviews at CNN Center in Atlanta.

I would like to express my deep appreciation to my family. My parents, William and Alice Richards, have also been supportive of me in all my endeavors. My daughter, Anne Elizabeth, a future author, constantly shows me the importance of getting one's ideas heard. My son, Matthew Ryan, who elevated the "terrible twos" to an art form, reminded me that free expression is alive and vibrant even in the middle of the night. And finally, a special word of thanks to a close family friend, Pam Ruest, Esquire, who has listened to my carrying on about the First Amendment over many a Saturday night dinner.

Robert D. Richards
State College, Pennsylvania

1

Sounding Freedom's Alarm

"Congress shall make no law respecting the establishment of religion, or prohibiting the free exercise thereof; or abridging the freedom of speech, or of the press; or the right of the people peaceably to assemble, and to petition the government for a redress of grievances."

— The First Amendment, 1791

One might very fairly question the need for another book on the First Amendment. After all, this constitutional provision has been around for over two hundred years, contains only forty-five words, and is as much a part of the fabric of the democracy as the concept of no taxation without representation, not to mention being the subject of countless books. Alas, a need does exist. Americans, now more than ever before, need to examine the notion of free speech in our society. Much has happened to the protection of expression in the past few decades. In some ways protection has been expanded, but in other significant ways it has been greatly reduced.

The main argument of this book is that the First Amendment is not afloat in a safe harbor. In fact, free speech is perhaps more under siege now than ever before in this country's history — certainly its recent history. What makes today's attack more insidious is that it comes from many segments of the society, from some unlikely assailants, and is often camouflaged in laudable fashion. Americans need to recognize this erosion of our fundamental liberty, but this is not an easy task. Attacks are cleverly disguised in attempts to increase free market enterprise, create nonhostile environments on college campuses, encourage decency or family values in the arts and entertainment industry, punish a newspaper that prints scathing comments about a public official, regulate what children see on television or their computer screens, protect a national symbol, and to conduct other praiseworthy endeavors.

The erosion has been a gradual one — hardly noticeable to the untrained eye — but very real in terms of the effects on everyone who calls America home. Accordingly, this book is designed secondarily as a survival manual for the First Amendment. By exposing some open wounds on the body of free speech, this book can help citizens do what they need to do to save this constitutional right from further infection. Some readers by now may be skeptical of the alarmist tone already adopted. Read on. The chapters that follow will present the case for the alarm to ring — and ring loudly.

The book will be in vain, however, if Americans refuse to once again embrace the notion of free speech as a positive and necessary feature for society. Doing so requires an enormous commitment by all of us to transcend the often-despicable factual situations requiring First Amendment assistance. Two hundred years of hard-fought challenges to free expression are now too often forgotten in the political cause célèbre of the moment. Moreover, America now faces a crisis of complaisance that threatens to overtake expressive liberty if we are not vigilant.

We have often looked to those who benefit most by the First Amendment — notably the media and even government — for leadership and this critical vigilance. Yet both camps have been negligent in this sacred duty, and the situation is worsening. News organizations that used to pursue the cause of the First Amendment, if only for the sake of principle, now back down — even when the outcome affects their day-to-day operations — for no other reason than the bottom line. Government officials think nothing of using the status of their office to place pressure on communicators to change their message (for example, television programming offensive to certain segments of society). When covering the transgressions on expression by courts or the legislatures, the media, instead of shouting foul,

13

trot out their lawyers, who say, "It's really not that bad" or "It could have been worse." The latter comment is hardly profound, and the former is really untrue.

The chipping away of free speech principles causes severe consequences — maybe not immediately but clearly over time. Restrictions on speech have a domino effect. For example, let us say that the United States Supreme Court rules that opinions printed in newspapers or published electronically are not immune from libel suits (as it did in the 1990 case of *Milkovich v. Lorain Journal Co.*). Before that 1990 decision, it was generally accepted law that opinions published in such places as columns, editorials, op-eds, and reviews were generally immune from libel suits. After all, such remarks were just someone's opinion, clearly recognized as such, and not an expression of facts sullying someone's reputation. If the aggrieved party brought the opinion piece to the attention of an attorney, the wise lawyer would be sympathetic but would diplomatically explain that the law recognizes a distinction between fact and opinion. The lawyer might also suggest framing a response in terms of a letter to the editor rather than a lawsuit; that is, counter the speech with more speech.

Milkovich changed that. Despite the nonalarmists' claim that the decision was not that bad, lawsuits have arisen out of the case, and defamation law has been muddled by it. Shortly after *Milkovich*, a Washington, D.C., author filed a lawsuit in federal court against the New York Times Company claiming that his reputation was defiled in a review of his latest book by the *New York Times Book Review*. A favorable review in the *Times Book Review* can help make an author's career; an unfavorable review can break it. The author called the *Milkovich* case a godsend. The author's case took nearly five years to resolve. In the end, the *New York Times* prevailed, but the defense was costly in terms of both dollars and time expended. Had it not been for the *Milkovich* case, the lawsuit against the *Times* probably would not have been filed, or at least might not have taken so long to resolve. (The effects of the *Milkovich* decision will be explored further in chapter seven.)

Other such cases followed. Critics face tough times because the Supreme Court ruled that opinions based on incorrect or incomplete facts or an erroneous assessment of facts could be actionable. Americans rely on critics to help us make decisions in terms of the movies, books, plays, or restaurants on which we want to spend our money. That speech is now tempered by the pall of a possible lawsuit. This is an admittedly minor problem in the greater scheme of public discourse, but the purpose in mentioning it here is to illustrate the problems associated with chipping away at established free speech rights. Moreover, the ripple effect will also be seen in cases of political and social opinion.

The chapters that follow present more heinous examples of the erosion of liberty — ones with greater consequences for the democratic landscape.

CAUSE FOR ALARM

The First Amendment was created essentially to protect unpopular views, to allow criticism of the government, to enable religious freedom, and to give citizens, both individually and collectively, a voice in governing. Yet many citizens today question whether this right should extend to those who burn a national symbol, put a crucifix upside down in urine, rally outside an abortion clinic, tell all on a daytime talk show, or seek to reveal the gruesome details of a celebrity murder case. The opponents of such expression are often outspoken and include some powerful people. This collective wisdom can be looked on as a type of tyranny of the majority.

It is very easy to champion majority views, and, in reality, we do not need a constitution to accomplish such a task. That is precisely why the Constitution was *not* written to protect majority viewpoints. Quite to the contrary, the First Amendment exists to protect expression by the minority. The founders were keenly aware of majoritarian thinking. After all, rebelling against authority got them where they were in the first place. Revolution is not typically the handiwork of proponents of the status quo. Today, the outspoken majority has been successful in watering down free expression with public support (in some cases, enthusiastic support) by championing a noble cause such as cleaning up daytime television. The tactic is rarely looked on as having anything to do with the First Amendment because, in many cases, no direct government intervention is involved. Rather, the result comes from an insidious chill on expression. Focusing on the ugly subject of a particular talk show diverts attention from the underlying beauty, if not the necessity, of having the right to air the topic in the first place.

Indeed, in order to enjoy our own free speech rights protected by the First Amendment, we must be willing to tolerate other views. The sacrifice has proved over and over to be worth it. Throughout history the First Amendment has been central to advances in religious freedom, civil rights, opening government to the people, and bringing down demagogues such as Joseph McCarthy. Today, abuses against the First Amendment rights of citizens and others whose livelihood or craft depends on the protections are manifold. Here are just some examples.

- In an alarming trend, citizens who are concerned about their neighborhoods and show up at a zoning hearing to oppose a development project too often find themselves defendants in multimillion-dollar lawsuits. The developers claim that these citizens have defamed them or wrongly interfered with their businesses. The citizens have to hire an attorney to defend rights guaranteed under the petition clause of the First Amendment. The goal of the businesses is met merely by filing suit. They get to retaliate against the citizens who spoke out and to warn the others to stay away — a double benefit for them. The problem has become so widespread that the acronym SLAPP, standing for Strategic Lawsuits Against Public Participation, has been attached. Several states have passed anti-SLAPP laws protecting citizens in these actions, but a strong business lobby has prevented such measures in many other states.

- On college campuses, students, faculty, and staff have been stifled by the political correctness (PC) movement and its aftermath. Speech codes proscribing various forms of expression have been labeled as part of a "new McCarthyism." These codes have resulted in many students' being taunted and unfairly singled out by administrators seeking to prove they are doing all they can to create a nonhostile environment for all students. In some cases, when unfavorable speech has appeared in

18

campus newspapers, the periodicals have been stolen or destroyed. Those who work and study on college campuses no longer feel safe in expressing views that may be perceived as non-PC. The pressure is subtle, but it threatens to undermine the central mission of the university. The result is a chilling of expression across campuses.

- Additionally, the arts and entertainment industries continue to be a hotbed of controversy, again with the First Amendment at the center. The 1990s opened with museum officials on trial for obscenity for exhibiting the erotic photograph collection of artist Robert Mapplethorpe and with rappers on trial for performing a song called "As Nasty As They Wanna Be," also alleged to be obscene. These cases touched off a debate in Congress over federal funding for the arts. Opponents of arts funding like to blur the real issues with rhetoric over using taxpayer dollars to fund indecent works. They overlook the benefit of arts education and the economic benefit to government support of the arts. Congress has also once again taken on the television industry, looking for a ratings system to help parents make informed choices for programming for their children. The industry responded, but many in Congress are not yet pleased with the result.

- At the same time, the lines of distinction

between entertainment and information are blurring. Tabloid news or pseudonews shows are bundled in with traditional news programs. The proliferation of daytime talk shows with tell-all guests calls into question, for some, the role of free speech in society, particularly after one such show led to the murder of one guest by another. Talk radio shows also contribute to the American dialogue sometimes with irreverent or hateful views.

- Monetary verdicts against media organizations have soared in the 1990s. In the first two years of this decade alone, juries awarded twenty-one judgments totaling $190.4 million in damages in libel cases. That figure includes six verdicts that topped $10 million each. Compare the amounts for 1990 and 1991 with the total for the entire decade of the 1980s — $231.9 million. Compare all those figures with the largest verdict ever — $222.7 million, levied in March 1997 — and there can be no doubt that jurors are sending the media a message. Although many, if not most, of these judgments do not stand up on appeal, the cost of defending these cases has a chilling effect on the types of stories news organizations undertake. Henry Kaufman, the general counsel for the Libel Defense Resource Center, summed up the situation this way: "The potential targets of overzealous awards are not simply the wallets of publishers and their insurers but all those dependent on the protection of their unfettered expression under the First Amendment."

News organizations are not only being slugged by juries in defamation cases, but smart lawyers are using other reasons to sue — ones that permit an end run around established First Amendment defenses.

- Earlier this decade, Court TV made its appearance on many of the nation's cable systems and proved that the country's fascination with the law is real in every sense of the word. The popularity of Court TV was helped along by some celebrated criminal cases, including the rape trial of William Kennedy Smith, the double murder charges against the Menendez brothers, and the O. J. Simpson case. Not only has Court TV carved out its niche in American jurisprudence, but CNN, C-SPAN, and the extended coverage of other networks and stations now occupy a place in the debate over bench-bar-media relations. The reporting also raises a fundamental conflict between the First Amendment's guarantee of a free press and the Sixth Amendment's right of the accused to a fair trial.
- The emergence and convergence of new technologies promise to forever change the

way information is distributed in this country. Information content has long been the bedrock on which First Amendment protection is based. Yet, traditionally, the delivery system has played a role, as evidenced by the degree of First Amendment protection afforded to newspapers as opposed to broadcasters over the decades. The Telecommunications Act of 1996 watered down First Amendment protections on the Internet and now has raised a whole new set of concerns about the blurring of the line between traditional print and electronic delivery systems.

- The First Amendment can also be found in the forefront of the movement to clean up the way election campaigns are financed. Because of a Supreme Court decision in the 1970s that equated money with speech in political campaigns, any effort to cap expenditures runs afoul of the First Amendment. As a result, some members of Congress are quick to use the First Amendment as a convenient excuse for not reforming the system.

These and many other issues will be explored in depth in the pages that follow. The stories of people affected and those who have influence will be told. This book will unravel the legal concepts involved and present a holistic picture of the general health of the First Amendment.

2

Squelching Political Participation

"Short of a gun to the head, a greater threat to First Amendment expression can scarcely be imagined."

— *Gordon v. Marrone*, 1992

Betty Blake remembers learning in school about her right of free speech. So when a local developer wanted to bulldoze the beech trees that lined her Wantagh, New York, neighborhood to put up more houses, she organized her neighbors and spoke out against the project. They tied red ribbons around the trees and hung a bedsheet across Betty's lawn with the message "This neighborhood will not be terra-ized," playing on the developer's name, Terra Homes, Inc. Her movement caught the attention of both the local media and many residents of her Long Island community.

Betty fondly recalled her astonishment one night, early on in the campaign to save the serene surroundings of her neighborhood, when she and her neighbors were having a strategy meeting. The group had announced plans for a candlelight vigil following the get-together. "While we were having the meeting, I was hearing this roar outside, and when I got outside, I found a couple of hundred people milling around the street with candles," she recalled. Not all the events surrounding her movement, however, were quite as inspiring. She also recalled the threats and harassing phone calls warning her to abandon opposition to the project. She surmised the calls came from subcontractors who would benefit from the development.

This may help explain why Betty was reluctant to attend a meeting about the project held in the Wantagh town hall, but she feared that if she and her neighbors did not show, the project would go forward unopposed. So, at the suggestion of the municipality's presiding supervisor, she and some neighbors went. During the meeting, an attendance sheet was passed around. Shortly thereafter, Betty discovered something about exercising the right of free speech that she had not learned in school. "The developer and his lawyer got the attendance sheet, and they just did a regular dragnet," Betty said. "They sued almost everybody on the list, even people who were coming out for the first time and had done nothing except come, at my request, to the meeting."

Terra Homes, Inc., sued Betty and several of

her neighbors for $6.5 million, claiming they had defamed the company, interfered with business, and trespassed on private property. When Blake was served with the court papers, she put them aside at first, but her neighbors were "very, very upset." "It took me about three months to realize how much damage this lawsuit was doing," Blake added. "Every meeting we go to, we're not talking about the trees anymore, we're talking about the lawsuit." The suit was filed in August, and by January several of her neighbors had caved in to the developer's pressures, had abandoned the campaign, and had been dismissed from the lawsuit. The remaining three told Betty that they could not get out of the lawsuit unless they convinced her to take down her signs. Betty said the neighbors implored her, "Why don't you take them down just for a little while, Betty, so I can get out of the lawsuit, and then you can put them up again, if you want." Blake refused to remove her signs and be "held hostage" by the developer. Eventually, the three neighbors were dismissed from the lawsuit, leaving Betty as the sole target.

The situation in Wantagh is a classic example of what has become a national legal phenomenon — businesses suing citizens to stop them from speaking out against a particular project. The Political Litigation Project at the University of Denver has coined the descriptive term SLAPP — Strategic Lawsuits Against Public Participation. Thousands of citizens, just like

Betty Blake, have been sued in recent years. And as the University of Denver's George Pring, one of the original researchers on the topic, points out, "It's just the tip of the iceberg." Lawmakers are beginning to take notice of this abusive legal tactic. Nine states have enacted laws protecting citizens sued for speaking out. New York had one of the first laws — thanks, in part, to Betty Blake's cause célèbre.

States with high levels of land-use activity run the greatest risk of SLAPPs. After learning about SLAPPs through news reports, Florida's attorney general, Robert A. Butterworth, directed his staff to look into their prevalence in the Sunshine State. Diana Sawaya-Crane, who ran the study, said that her office identified twenty-one cases just by contacting environmental and citizen's groups. She, too, realized that many more SLAPPs exist. Often, citizens who are sued do not realize the case has been filed in an effort to stifle their legitimate expression.

Another difficulty in identifying SLAPPs is that the lawsuits are filed on a variety of grounds. "For the most part, when they file these suits, they are filed under a number of different torts [civil wrongs] — interference, slander, libel, conspiracy — and they don't say this is a SLAPP suit that we're filing," Sawaya-Crane said. She added that when courts, lawyers, and citizens themselves are unaware that the case amounts to a SLAPP, they miss the opportunity to mount a

First Amendment defense. "Many people just try to defend it in the traditional way of defending a civil case, as opposed to going to the heart of the case, which is intimidation of citizens to keep them from continuing to voice their concerns," she said. Despite attempts by some state legislators, Florida has yet to enact a law protecting citizens from such intimidation suits.

No state law, however, can erase the emotional turmoil felt by SLAPP targets. Kenny and Tammy Rucker of Point of Rocks, Maryland, experienced the stress associated with a SLAPP suit for almost two years. Their story began when a trash hauler sought to bring in waste from outside Frederick County to a site in the tiny community of Point of Rocks. Free State Recycling Systems, Inc., filed for permits to operate a solid waste–processing firm in the community.[1] The firm planned to haul in refuse from neighboring counties as well as from New York, New Jersey, and Virginia. The company would then remove the recyclable materials for sale and dump the rest in landfills outside Frederick County, although residents feared this would not be the case.

The couple joined with their neighbors to form a community action group to oppose the hauling operation. The group called itself H.I.T., short for Halt Imported Trash. H.I.T. members immediately began a campaign to stop the construction of the recycling facility. The group alleged that Free State had violated several local and state laws. Specifically, they discovered that Free State had begun construction without the required permits and that county officials had done nothing to stop it.[2] When H.I.T. organizers decided to send a letter to some 475 Point of Rocks residents on August 23, 1991, Tammy recalled one member's asking her if she was afraid of being sued. "How can you be sued for exercising your First Amendment right?" she replied. But Free State's attorney claimed the group was spreading "misinformation." When the suit was filed, Tammy remembered thinking, "Oh, my God, this can't be true." The letter, signed by "Concerned Residents of Frederick County," became the basis for the lawsuit. Specifically, Charles O'Brien, an executive of Free State, objected to what he termed "false and defamatory statements":

Free State is not supposed to dump out-of-county trash in the Frederick County landfill. Mr. Charles O'Brien, one of the owners of Free State, was the owner of a waste-hauling company called LCCC, located in Montgomery County, MD. LCCC trucks from this facility were caught trying to dump trash out of county illegally in the Frederick County landfill. Mr. O'Brien sold his interest in the facility after the citations for illegal dumping were issued.

The Frederick County Commissioners have not required Free State to post a performance bond. If the company declares bankruptcy the County will have no security to pay for site clean-up and any contamination problems. Mr. O'Brien, one of Free State's owners, filed for bankruptcy six times in 1986, according to Frederick County records. If the operation of Free State results in the contamination of the groundwater or surface waters, and the company files for bankruptcy, the citizens of Frederick County could end up shouldering the burden for the company's failure.[3]

The Ruckers were never named in the lawsuit. Instead, the trash hauler used a typical SLAPP tactic of suing one (or more) person (in this case, the person who had paid for the letter's postage) and "100 John Does." The addition of the John Does is designed to intimidate the others. It notifies the court that additional parties may be added once they are identified. Consequently, in the SLAPP context, this procedural device also serves as a warning to other citizens in the community that they, too, may be added as a party to the lawsuit.

"I looked at it as being a way to silence people, and it was very effective," Tammy said. "You list one hundred John Does, and you think of this community as small as it is, and, well geez, that's just about everybody." The tactic also allows the lawsuit's filer to conduct extensive discovery (a pretrial mechanism in which parties obtain information from each other), such as depositions.

The Ruckers got involved in the trash-hauling issue because they wanted to do what they thought was best for their community. The community's water needs were served by two large wells, and the residents feared the landfill would pollute the water supply. The property on which the facility was to be located was within the 100-year flood plain and streams that emptied into the Potomac River and either abutted or crossed the Free State property.[4] As Tammy put it, "We wanted to raise our families here. This is not a place to have a revolving landfill." Tammy's views reflect the NIMBY (Not In My Back Yard) syndrome. Because of their involvement, the Ruckers fully expected to be named in the lawsuit. H.I.T. members were systematically served with deposition notices while participating in public functions. "We had a community cleanup day where we were working on a [playground], and one of the principal officers [of H.I.T.] was served at that day," Kenny Rucker observed. At the depositions, the lawyer questioning the citizens asked several questions about the value of H.I.T. members' homes and the types of jobs they had. As Kenny Rucker recognized, "It was an intimidation ploy."

When the Ruckers were served, they immediately contacted their homeowners' insurance company and found that their policy provided no coverage for such lawsuits. Their neighbors experienced similar results. "Without fail, every [homeowners'] insurance company — and there were several different ones involved — none of them provided coverage for this kind of lawsuit," Kenny observed. As a result, as news of the lawsuit spread, community support for H.I.T. withered. "Immediately, we lost about fifty percent of our membership, and our fundraising slowed to a trickle," Kenny noted.

The deposition notices kept coming, and the intimidating questions continued. It got so bad that the Frederick County trial judge finally halted the depositions and threw out the lawsuit. The trash hauler appealed, but the lower court's judgment was upheld. But winning the lawsuit is not the goal of those who file SLAPPs. Rather, the goal is to use intimidation tactics to throw an organized effort off balance, if not dissolve it completely. The businesses involved are keenly aware that the citizens they target do not have the financial resources to maintain a defense. When the Ruckers were served with a deposition notice and the fear of being named in the lawsuit became intense, they panicked. "We started exploring what we could do to protect our home, because we have three children — at the time, all preschool age," Kenny noted. "We started changing over title."

The lawsuit took its personal toll as well. Tammy would be sitting in their living room and, all at once, begin to cry when she thought about the lawsuit. Said Kenny, "It caused some real hardship on our personal relationship, our marriage, because there's different opinions about what we should do and how we should protect what we've got." The long-term effects are serious, too. As a local union officer, Kenny said he's used to controversy, but Tammy's willingness to get involved in issues has waned severely. "My wife will not step out into the community spotlight at all now to take up a cause. She even questions charitable organizations," Kenny explained.

University of Denver sociologist Penelope Canan, who coined the term SLAPP, found that Tammy Rucker's reaction is typical. Canan said SLAPP targets routinely report that the lawsuit is "one of the most life changing experiences they have ever had."[5] The legal gymnastics they are put through often translate into physical problems. And although the physiological disorders associated with SLAPP are similar to those connected to other stress-related illnesses, one social behavior is peculiar to SLAPP: "the demise of the belief in American justice." Canan also found that after being SLAPPed — or even after just learning about such law suits — citizens are less likely to become involved in public issues. This factor is significant, says Canan, because research has shown that only 10 percent of the public gets involved in the first place. People who experience SLAPP are not shocked by this finding.

The Ruckers' friends Chris and Jeff Arey can

understand their pain. They, too, were part of the Point of Rocks debacle. Chris said the lawsuit "caused a rift between the whole community as far as who was at fault . . . a lot of finger pointing." It led to an even greater degree of apathy among the citizens there. The Areys now understand why people don't want to get involved in community issues. "We did go through a lot of stressed-out periods and a lot of concern when they say they are suing you for a quarter million dollars each, and you are barely paying bills," Chris lamented. They now "think twice" anytime they think about becoming involved in a public issue. Jeff Arey has testified before Maryland's House of Delegates in an effort to get an anti-SLAPP law passed in that state, but thus far the bill has never made it out of committee.

Another Maryland couple has made several trips to the state capital for the same reason. Herb and Wink Jonas live in Havre de Grace, in rural Harford County. When the Jonases and their neighbors banded together to stop a proposed rubblefill, they, too, became defendants in a multimillion-dollar lawsuit, and they spent more than five years battling the company that wanted to construct the project. The Jonases opposed the rubblefill because they feared pollutants from it would cut further into the community's aquifers and jeopardize their already depleted water supply.

After the Jonases contacted environmental

officials about their concerns, the company sued them for just under $3 million. The suit alleged that the couple had defamed the company when they contacted officials and when they talked about the situation while looking up records in the courthouse. They were also sued for trespass and interference with business.

Wink Jonas, who said she had always been healthy, experienced physical problems because of the lawsuit. "My stomach got all upset, and I couldn't sleep a lot, and I was nervous," she said. But the Jonases SLAPPed back. They filed a countersuit for $6.7 million, alleging malicious abuse of process and intentional infliction of emotional distress.

The businesses that file SLAPPs contend that they are simply exercising their right to use legal process to redress grievances. Although they acknowledge that individuals may not be happy with a project, they say developers have rights, too. SLAPP critics argue that the appropriate forum for resolving such disputes is the hearing room of the local zoning board or county council — not the courtroom. Moreover, SLAPPs are not limited to zoning disputes. People have been sued for complaining to a school board about the competence of a teacher, for reporting violations to environmental and consumer authorities, for drawing attention to police misconduct and child abuse, and even for writing letters to the editor.

HISTORICAL UNDERPINNINGS

One of the primary legal difficulties surrounding SLAPPs is the erosion of constitutional rights encompassed in such litigation. This nation's founders placed a high value on the ability of the people to have access to their government. This notion of making imperative the right of the citizenry to communicate with its government is central to a democracy, and as a result, the drafters of the First Amendment included a provision protecting the right of the people "to petition the Government for a redress of grievances." Petitioning necessarily embraces the ability to convey any information a citizen believes to be important to a governmental unit. Yet the United States Supreme Court has been reluctant to apply any comprehensive immunity to remarks made by citizens in this regard.

In 1981, when a North Carolina state judge was under consideration for United States Attorney, Robert McDonald wrote two letters to President Reagan, sending duplicate copies to other members of the president's administration. Judge Smith contended in court papers that the letters "falsely accused [him] of 'violating the civil rights of various individuals while a Superior Court judge,' 'fraud and conspiracy to commit fraud,' 'extortion or blackmail,' and 'violations of professional ethics.' "[6] Smith was not appointed to the federal post. In court, McDonald defended by arguing that the petition clause of the First Amendment provided absolute immunity from liability. When the case reached the United States Supreme Court, the justices disagreed with McDonald's contention.

The Court recognized that the First Amendment's right to petition the government is "cut from the same cloth as other guarantees of that Amendment, and is an assurance of a particular freedom of expression," but said it does not relieve citizens from liability arising out of it.[7] Writing for the Court, Chief Justice Burger said, "Although the values and right of petition as an important aspect of self-government are beyond question, it does not follow that the framers of the First Amendment believed that the petition clause provided absolute immunity from damage for libel."[8]

In his concurring opinion, Justice Brennan, joined by Justices Marshall and Blackmun, agreed that no *absolute* immunity exists but stressed that *qualified* immunity, as directed by Brennan's landmark opinion in *New York Times Co. v. Sullivan*,[9] should apply.[10] In 1964, Brennan nationalized libel law with respect to criticism of public officials concerning their official capacities by allowing recovery of damages only if public officials can prove, by clear and convincing evidence, that the defamatory statement was made with actual malice. This means that the speaker knew the statement was false when he or she made it or else made it with reckless disregard of its falsity.[11] "Reckless disregard" has been interpreted to mean that the speaker entertained serious doubt about the truth of the remarks he or she was making.

Despite the Supreme Court's explicit denial of immunity in petition clause cases, lower courts across the country have focused attention on the chilling effect of SLAPPs and have allowed, in some cases, early dismissal, sanctions, and even SLAPP-back suits. SLAPP-backs are filed by SLAPP defendants alleging abuse of process and/or malicious prosecution, effectively charging that the plaintiff filed the original suit in bad faith. SLAPP-backs have found moderate success.

Consider, for example, the case of three California growers who purchased newspaper advertisements accusing the J. G. Boswell Co. of opposing a proposed canal in an effort to create a monopoly for itself in cotton farming. The growers also accused the company of trying to use a ballot measure to secure cheap water for itself. The company sued the growers for libel, but a jury found the claim baseless and awarded the growers $3 million in general damages (later reduced to $600,000) and $10.5 million in punitive damages on a malicious prosecution counterclaim. The verdict held up on appeal, and the state's highest court let the judgment stand by refusing to hear the case.[12]

In the Maryland case involving the Ruckers

and the Areys, the trial judge recognized the motivation behind the lawsuit. In announcing her ruling from the bench, Frederick County Circuit Judge Mary Ann Stepler said, "I think that in this case there is no question that in fact it is a SLAPP suit."[13] Yet, such a finding by a judge is unusual. SLAPPs are not commonly understood, even in legal circles, and they are even more difficult to locate and identify.

The University of Denver's Political Litigation Project has tracked thousands of cases in the past decade, but the precise number of SLAPP actions is impossible to identify because these lawsuits rarely go beyond the trial court level. Trial courts do not ordinarily publish opinions or rulings. Moreover, as the Florida Attorney General's report showed, these suits masquerade as traditional lawsuits in defamation, tortious interference, civil rights, and other actions. Consequently, only after careful analysis of the factual background of these cases can the SLAPP nature of the action be recognized. Even in those cases that reach the appellate level, judges are sometimes reluctant to break new ground and create special treatment for SLAPP cases. In the Point of Rocks case, despite the trial court's explicit finding that the lawsuit was a SLAPP, the appellate court said such a finding was "unnecessary to its decision and our affirmance on appeal." In other words, the higher court was able to reach the same result as the court below without a "determination that

[O'Brien] brought the suit to harass the persons opposed to Free State's recycling facility."[14]

IDENTIFYING SLAPPS

Despite the dearth of appellate dispositions, some patterns have emerged from the reported decisions. Courts at all levels are beginning to gain awareness of the SLAPP phenomenon and the SLAPP label, but education is a slow process. This point was illustrated in the New York case of *Gordon v. Marrone*.[15] The Nature Conservancy had become a thorn in the side of real estate developer Allen S. Gordon. The group had opposed Gordon's plan to subdivide a 36-acre tract of undeveloped property located near the Conservancy's Mianus River Gorge Wildlife Refuge and Botanical Preserve. In retaliation for the opposition, Gordon sought an annulment of the real estate tax exemption enjoyed by the Conservancy for a house it owned across from its 569-acre refuge and preserve. Gordon focused his suit against the town assessor, Anna Maria Marrone, on the fact that the house was occupied by the Conservancy's executive director and her family. Yet the house also served as the preserve's administrative center.

The judge recognized that Gordon had no injury for which to sue and thus agreed with the Conservancy's characterization of the action as a SLAPP. His opinion spelled out the lawsuit's retaliatory motive.

Given the absence of any apparent real pecuniary benefit to the petitioner from this litigation, if he were successful, the Court can only conclude that petitioner's motivation is that ascribed to him by the Conservancy — retribution against the Conservancy for opposing his development plans for the area around the Mianus Gorge, and an effort to chill the Conservancy's future exercise of its First Amendment rights.[16]

As was noted earlier, the goal in a SLAPP is not winning the lawsuit. The lawsuit's purpose is realized through the process. Causing problems for the SLAPP target is the actual goal — depositions, interrogatories, wondering what is next all contribute to a state of heightened anxiety and often cause a retreat from public opposition to the filer's project.

In an effort to classify these lawsuits, the Political Litigation Project developed a four-part test for determining if a lawsuit is a SLAPP. The suit must be:

1. A civil claim for money damages
2. Filed against nongovernmental individuals and organizations
3. Based on advocacy before a governmental branch official or the electorate, and/or

4. A substantive issue of some public or societal significance[17]

This definition is flexible enough to encompass the myriad situations in which SLAPPs have arisen, yet it does little to aid the location of such lawsuits. Classification may improve as courts begin to adopt the SLAPP label as the previously mentioned decisions did. In the meantime, recognized SLAPPs provide enough common elements to help identification. One such element is a business that was unsuccessful in a controversial battle in a political arena and is now seeking retribution and compensation through litigation. *SRW Associates v. Bellport Beach Property Owners* provides a typical SLAPP scenario.[18] SRW Associates sought approval of a cluster development subdivision plan by the town board of Brookhaven, on Long Island. The town's planning board had already approved the application, but civic organizations quickly embarked on a publicity campaign opposing the plan. They hoped to stir public opposition in an effort to "preserve the existing character of the residential neighborhood."[19] The statements made by officers of these organizations were both oral and written. Some of these statements were repeated by the media. They called the developer's project "clustered condominiums" and "multiple housing." The application, in reality, sought approval for the clustering of thirty-six separate single-family units, not apartment units as the statements suggested.

The adverse publicity led to a public hearing at which several hundred residents demonstrated their opposition to the plan. SRW's zoning application was denied. This caused the developer to sue the neighborhood groups, alleging that "its application was denied because of the overwhelming community objections brought about solely as a result of false and misleading statements of the defendants, which created the impression that the plaintiff sought to erect multiple dwelling structures rather than individual residential units."[20]

Trying to link the denial of its application to the statements made by residents in opposition to the project proved futile for the developer. In ruling for the residents, the court observed:

We find that, as a matter of law, there was no causation between the alleged misrepresentation published by the defendants to the members of the public prior to the hearing and the town board's denial of the plaintiff's application. There is no allegation that materially false statements were uttered by the defendants to the town board at the public hearing. The minutes of the public hearing, which were attached to the motion papers, undisputedly show that the plaintiff's subdivision proposal for cluster zoning of detached single-family residences was accurately represented to the town board and to members of

42

the public who attended the hearing by an attorney and architect retained by the plaintiff.[21]

The *SRW Associates* case illustrates what typically happens in SLAPP situations. The battle should take place in the political forum designed for such discussions, such as the zoning hearing board. In such instances, both sides have a chance to air their concerns. The typical SLAPP arises, however, when the unsuccessful business enterprise wants to settle the score in court. By merely filing the lawsuit, the business is able to assume the advantage. The citizens now have to obtain legal representation to defend themselves. The costs associated with counsel are often enough to silence the opposition. Even though the citizens eventually win dismissal of the case, as in the *SRW Associates* action, where the court found no "reasonable basis to support a finding" that the residents' statements "were a cause-in-fact of the denial of its application by the town board,"[22] the trauma and costs of the litigation make the citizens (and the First Amendment rights at stake) the ultimate loser.

When people become emotional in an attempt to preserve the character of their neighborhood, they sometimes resort to offhand remarks. SLAPP filers capitalize on these indiscretions as the basis for their lawsuits. In law, such remarks are generally considered "rhetorical hyperbole," and as such are not defamatory and are fully protected by the First Amendment. Nonetheless, the determination of whether such remarks are defamatory or mere hyperbole must be made in court. Edith Hull, a local political activist in Cecil County, Maryland, learned this lesson the hard way.

When local businessman and occasional politician Warwick Sherrard filed an application to change the zoning designation of his property near her farm, she opposed it in testimony before the county board of commissioners. After learning that the board had approved Sherrard's application, Hull went to an open meeting of the board and said to a commissioner who had voted in favor of the rezoning application, "I would like to know how much money it cost Warwick."[23] This remark prompted Sherrard to file a lawsuit claiming he had been defamed. A jury found in favor of Edith Hull, but Sherrard appealed. Maryland's appellate court upheld the verdict in Hull's favor, saying:

[R]emarks made by an individual in the course of petitioning for a redress of grievances before a legislative body are absolutely privileged under the First Amendment to the United States Constitution. So long as the individual's comments are not part of a sham and are relevant to his petition and thus are uttered as part of or in conjunction with it, he may not be held liable in damages for defamation.[24]

This would have been a great victory for the First Amendment rights of citizens to participate in governmental affairs, but *Sherrard v. Hull* was heard two years prior to the United States Supreme Court decision in *McDonald* (discussed earlier in this chapter), where the Court refused to recognize the privilege the Maryland court thought had existed.

Even correspondence to government officials has been the basis of a SLAPP. In *Walters v. Linhof*, a group of citizens in Colorado sent letters to the El Paso County Land Use Department in which they labeled a developer "a land option speculator posing as a developer" and said, "We have reason to urge that the County Commissioners examine thoroughly the financial capability and technical knowledge of this developer."[25] Another letter was sent to a newspaper and was published as a letter to the editor. It read, "I was shocked to learn that many of the California towns where Walters claimed to have experience were familiar to me. My thoughts wandered to overbuilt and crowded subdivisions, run-down and vacant shopping centers, and industrial complexes which are real eyesores."[26]

Walters sued in federal court for defamation, claiming that these letters injured his reputation as a developer. The district judge disagreed, finding no defamatory content to the letters.

Read as a whole and in their ordinary meaning, these statements do not hold plaintiffs up to hatred, contempt or ridicule. Plaintiffs may not pull statements out of context to conjure up a defamatory meaning as they have here attempted to do. The statements do not injure the reputation or character of the plaintiffs. I recognize that in the arena of politics these statements may contribute to a decision which is adverse to plaintiffs' plans for the construction project, but economic advantage is not the legal equivalent of reputation.[27]

The more lasting importance of this decision came in a sentence in which the judge recognized the critical nature of public participation in government. He said, "Public hearings and free and open communication by citizens with public agencies and public officials give the First Amendment its raison d'être."[28]

LETTERS TO THE EDITOR

The *Walters* case was based, in part, on a letter to the editor. Such open letters have provided the impetus for other SLAPP suits. In Piscataway, New Jersey, a developer purchased a former school property that many residents thought was underappraised. Residents vocalized their discontent in letters to the *P.D. Review*, a newspaper serving the local area. The developer sued, claiming his reputation had been injured. The court sympathized with the developer's worry about his reputation but was more concerned about the chilling effect that such lawsuits have on public discourse. The trial court found the letters were expressions of "pure opinion" and not actionable. The New Jersey appellate court agreed, saying opinions expressed "even in the most colorful and hyperbolic terms" deserve protection.[29]

The court's opinion captured the essence of the SLAPP and promised a heightened standard of review in such cases.

> We nevertheless fear that no one will be left to carry the torch of criticism even when defendants like those in this case are vindicated, after they have withstood the financial and emotional rigors of litigation such as this. Indeed it may become too costly for ordinary citizens to exercise the right of free speech which undergirds a democratic society. We are profoundly concerned with the chilling effect that plaintiffs' lawsuit in these rather unremarkable circumstances may have on other citizens who ordinarily speak out on behalf of what they perceive to be the public good.[30]

Although this New Jersey court demonstrated insight into the motivations behind SLAPP actions, many judges are unaware, at first glance, that interference with a constitutional right is at issue. It is important to recall that SLAPP targets are engaged in constitutionally protected activity, such as free speech or petitioning the government for a redress of grievances. Most times, because of the protected nature of the activity, no viable claim exists for the filer, and the lawsuit serves only to harass. Moreover, the name-calling and emotionally charged language that often form the basis of these actions is enveloped in the category of "rhetorical hyperbole" and thus is not compensable in most situations. Despite the safeguards accorded by the federal and state constitutions, the prevalence of SLAPPs has prompted legislatures in nine states to pass specific protections for citizens, and other states are getting into the act.

RESPONSE BY THE STATES

Despite the efforts of people like the Jonases, the Areys, and the Ruckers, anti-SLAPP legislation has not progressed very far in Maryland. A bill was introduced on January 23, 1992, specifically characterizing this type of lawsuit as a Strategic Lawsuit Against Public Participation and providing damages for the SLAPP targets if they could demonstrate that the action was inspired by intimidation or harassment purposes. Two months later, however, Bill No. 486 was reported unfavorably from the House Committee on Judiciary.

Betty Blake's state legislature was more sympathetic. New York's law, which became effective on January 1, 1993, amended the civil rights and civil practice laws and rules to protect the "rights of citizens to participate freely in the public process" and to "provide the utmost protection for the free exercise of speech, petition, and association rights, particularly where such rights are exercised in a public forum with respect to issues of public concern."[31] The legislature's rationale centered on the use of process for harassment and intimidation. Under New York's law a person sued in a SLAPP action may recover damages, costs, and attorney's fees if it can be shown that the action both involved public petitioning and had no "substantial basis in fact and law and could not be supported by a substantial argument for the extension, modification or reversal of existing law."[32] If the SLAPP target can show that the lawsuit was filed specifically to harass, intimidate, or obstruct First Amendment rights, punitive damages (damages designed solely to punish the wrongdoer) may also be awarded.

In a significant move, the New York State legislature sought to make it extremely difficult for SLAPP plaintiffs to maintain a lawsuit arising out of a citizen's right to petition the government. Borrowing from the United States Supreme Court's landmark defamation case,

New York Times Co. v. Sullivan, the law requires SLAPP plaintiffs to prove actual malice by clear and convincing evidence.[33] "Actual malice" is a legal term of art, and it does not mean ill will, spite, or hatred. People who make remarks with actual malice do so with knowledge of the statements' falsity or at least with reckless disregard of the falsity; that is, while entertaining serious doubt about the statements' truth. In the New York anti-SLAPP law, that translates to mean that plaintiffs must establish that the "communication which gives rise to the action was made with knowledge of its falsity or with reckless disregard of whether it was false, where the truth or falsity of such communication is material to the cause of action at issue."[34]

Like New York, California has had its share of recognized SLAPP suits. It nonetheless took several attempts to get legislation passed in that state. The bills that were introduced went further in treating the policy considerations underlying such measures while still providing a practical procedural remedy. The bills went through several iterations and were vetoed by former Governor George Deukmejian and Governor Pete Wilson before a bill eventually was signed into law on September 16, 1992.

The law's preamble recognizes the "disturbing increase" in lawsuits designed mainly to stifle the expression of individuals engaged in petitioning activities. It further recognizes the need for citizens to participate in "matters of public

50

significance." To protect those citizens, the law requires a court to dismiss the suit unless the plaintiff shows a "substantial probability of success" on the claim.[35] This provision is significant because it mandates dismissal of the unmeritorious case early on in the litigation process. Consequently, it undermines the goal of the SLAPP filer, which is to use protracted legal process to crush public opposition. These cases must be terminated quickly if the right to petition is to be safeguarded. Allowing SLAPP targets to recover damages and attorneys' fees is another way to level the playing field for the citizens involved in these actions.

In Washington State, immunity attaches to communications made to a governmental agency. The law provides that "a person who in good faith communicates a complaint or information to any agency of federal, state or local government regarding any matter reasonably of concern to that agency shall be immune from civil liability or claims based upon communication to the agency."[36] Moreover, the state's attorney general may intervene and defend the SLAPP targets. Protection for SLAPP defendants also comes in the form of an amendment to the rules of civil procedure that permits a party against whom a frivolous suit has been filed to recover "reasonable expenses, including fees of attorney, incurred in opposing such action, counterclaim, cross-claim, third party claims, or defense."[37] The crux of this amendment is that "[t]he judge shall consider all evidence presented at the time of the motion to determine whether the position of the nonprevailing party was frivolous and advanced without reasonable cause." This motion can be made by the prevailing party regardless of whether the disposition of the case was voluntary or involuntary.

Nine other states have now passed anti-SLAPP laws. They are Oklahoma, Nevada, Delaware, Rhode Island, Minnesota, Massachusetts, Nebraska, Tennessee, and Georgia. States that are bastions of land-use activity also show a concentration of SLAPP actions, but the business lobby in some of those areas has successfully blocked such legislation.

Consider, for example, the state of Florida's attempts to enact anti-SLAPP protection. Palm Beach County state representative Mimi McAndrews introduced legislation there for two years in a row that never made it past the committee level.[38] Bills have typically taken some time to pass in each of the states where laws have passed. Diana Sawaya-Crane of the attorney general's office predicted it would take five to ten years to get a measure through the Florida legislature. McAndrews, who is no longer in the Florida legislature, said it is unlikely Florida will see any such law "unless [a SLAPP] happens personally to a Republican in a powerful venue."

The major force against the legislation in Florida was a lobbying group representing small and big businesses called the Associated Industries of Florida (AIF). Shortly after the attorney general's office issued its report on SLAPPs, the group issued its own position paper against anti-SLAPP legislation. According to McAndrews, the report prepared by Associated Industries was "extremely misleading." The report countered each of the cases outlined in the attorney general's study and questioned the actual injuries to the targets of SLAPP. In the introduction, the Associated Industries report contended, "[I]t is debatable whether these cases present evidence of 'innocent' victims being harassed, or whether they in fact show innocent companies being harassed by individuals under the guise of free speech."[39] In a somewhat novel approach, the AIF report argued in favor of SLAPP suits, calling them a "benefit afforded by the legal system." As the threat of a lawsuit looms, people will be more likely to modify their behavior. According to the report, "If people have no incentive to monitor their behavior then the rights of everyone will be trampled upon."[40] Shortly after the state's report was released, AIF's vice president and general counsel, Jodi L. Chase, wrote to Florida's attorney general, Robert A. Butterworth, voicing the organization's concern "about the ramifications of any legislation that attempts to limit the ability of an injured corporate citizen to seek remedies from the judicial branch."

McAndrews said the AIF lobby launched the

most formidable campaign against the legislation, claiming that businesses' rights would be reduced under this measure. She tried to sit down with another lobbying force against the bill, the Association of Developers. She wanted to work with that group to develop a bill that would address some of its concerns as well, but according to McAndrews, "I couldn't get them to go that step." Even so that group did not present the major opposition to the measure; AIF did. "They went to a very great extent to defeat the bill," McAndrews said.

And it worked, much to the displeasure of Florida lawyer Thomas W. Reese, who himself was a target of a SLAPP. When he represented the Environmental Confederation of Southwest Florida in an administrative challenge to a permit that had been issued to a developer, he and his clients were sued for $6 million by the developer for tortious interference with a business relationship, civil conspiracy, and defamation. According to Reese, when he took the depositions of two top executives from the developers Cape Cave, he asked them if they had information that could prove that he or his clients were doing anything illegal in their administrative challenge to the permit. "They pretty much said, 'We didn't, but we just knew you had been doing something illegal and that we were going to do discovery and find out.' " After the plaintiffs could not present any facts to back up their case, the circuit judge granted summary judgment in Reese's and his clients' favor, saying that Cape Cave's lawsuit had "an obvious chilling effect" on the First Amendment right to petition the government.[41] But Reese's problems did not end there. Despite his victory in the case, which not only named his clients but also himself personally, he was dropped by his legal malpractice insurance carrier and has not been able to secure new coverage.

Other states with failed anti-SLAPP initiatives tried to apply varying degrees of protection in their bills. On January 21, 1992, Senate Bill No. 424 was introduced in the Virginia State Senate. Virginia's measure was instructive because it specifically labeled such actions as SLAPPs and indicated likely plaintiffs. The bill provided for summary dismissal of such cases "if the right to petition under the Virginia or United States Constitution is properly raised in defense of a claim, counterclaim or cross-claim which is (i) brought by a person who has applied for or obtained a permit, zoning change, license, lease, certificate or other entitlement for use or permission to act, or by an individual or entity with materially related interests, connection or affiliation (the claimant), (ii) brought against a non-governmental individual or entity (the respondent), and (iii) is based upon advocacy by the respondent and is directed toward the claimant."[42]

New Jersey's bill, providing "limited immunity from SLAPP suits, including the right to recover attorney's fees," died both times it was introduced.[43] Texas attempted to institute a procedure whereby summary judgment would be granted along with attorneys' fees unless the SLAPP plaintiff proved that the defendant's motivation in opposing the plaintiff in the underlying government proceeding was to harass or to injure the plaintiff and that the defendant did, in fact, injure the plaintiff. The legislation did not pass when it was first introduced in 1990, nor when it was reintroduced in 1993.[44] The Connecticut legislature also entertained legislation for the second time in 1993. Two senate bills and one house bill were designed specifically to address the SLAPP problem by preventing "suits brought as retaliation against the exercise of constitutionally protected rights." Then a senate bill was introduced in January that would "protect the right of the public to speak at public meetings without fear of retaliation by restricting Strategic Lawsuits Against Public Participation." None of these measures made it past committee stages.[45] In 1993, Tennessee unsuccessfully attempted to create an immunity from civil liability for any "person who communicates a complaint or information to any agency of federal, state, or local government regarding a matter of concern to that agency" unless the person knew the information was false or communicated it in reckless disregard of its falsity.[46] The bill was finally passed and signed into law on June 6, 1997.

Pennsylvania's measure would apply only when the statements made concerned environmental matters, and although an earlier version passed the house unanimously, the current bill was stalled in committee for two years.[47] On October 29, 1997, the measure passed in the Pennsylvania House of Representatives. Kansas, Maryland, Michigan, and Texas also have bills pending as this book goes to press.

Opponents to these measures argue that the right to sue is severely curtailed by such legislation. They contend that everyone is entitled to his or her day in court.

A NATIONAL RESPONSE

The inability of many states to get legislation passed — or, in some cases, even introduced — prompted a national movement to get congressional attention. The National Coalition Against SLAPPs, headquartered in California and coordinated by attorney Mark Goldowitz and Roanne Withers, calls itself a "grassroots organizing effort" to get federal anti-SLAPP legislation passed. The proposed legislation, which was drafted with the help of the University of Denver's Political Litigation Project, establishes a substantive right of immunity from suit for citizens whose acts are "in furtherance of the constitutional rights to petition, speech, association, and participation in government . . . regardless of intent or purpose, except where not genuinely aimed at procuring favorable government action, result, or outcome." This legislation would clearly minimize the impact of the Supreme Court's decision in *McDonald v. Smith*, discussed earlier in this chapter. Joining the fight for a federal response is a Washington, D.C.–based group called Americans for Legal Reform. Currently, both groups are looking for allies on the House and Senate Judiciary Committees.

SLAPPs are intended to stifle people's participation, mostly at the local level. Sometimes they accomplish this through the lawsuit and the resultant publicity; other times, it is accomplished through a settlement, which often contains an order prohibiting the parties to talk about the case. One lawsuit in Florida actually went further and issued an injunction against the citizen, Robin Malik, forbidding her "from any participation at any homeowners' meeting regarding any claims that she had made in the past as to the improper election of any board member or director by the homeowners' association." Malik could also not make any further comments about the directors of the homeowners' association. This was part of the agreed-upon settlement that was incorporated into a court order.[48] Malik said that a lack of funds to continue fighting forced her to settle the case and give up certain of her First Amendment rights "by agreement of the parties."[49]

SLAPPING THE MEDICAL COMMUNITY

Although the vast majority of SLAPPs filed in the United States involve environmental and land-use issues, other areas are not immune from the sweep of similar litigation. One of the more dangerous areas SLAPPs have invaded is the medical profession. Pharmaceutical companies, profit-driven clinics, and Health Maintenance Organizations (HMOs) have found SLAPPs to be a convenient way of silencing physician-critics. The effect of such lawsuits on open debate about new drugs, clinical practices, and health care generally could prove deadly. The problem is that, as with SLAPPs in other areas, the impact would be hard to prove. Finding out just how many physicians with something to say about these areas kept silent because of the threat of litigation would be a difficult, if not impossible, task.

One fact that can be proved is that these lawsuits exist. Consider, for instance, a lawsuit filed against Dr. George R. Schwartz. Dr. Schwartz is a specialist in emergency medicine, and in fact has become quite prominent in that field. In 1994, he wrote an editorial for a publication in that specialty called *Emergency Medicine News*. His editorial lamented how multicontract hospital groups were taking over the emergency medicine field and how cost-cutting measures by these profit-driven management companies were detrimental to the care physicians could provide as well as to the emergency medicine field as a whole. Corporate shareholders were guiding the bottom line. Although he did not mention a group by name, his article tracked the money trail of a "recent management group which has gone public." Coastal Physician Group, Inc., filed a libel suit against Dr. Schwartz based on this editorial.

The suit prompted the American Academy of Emergency Medicine to establish a First Amendment Rights Fund for Emergency Physicians. The reason for the fund is spelled out in the academy's literature: "How many people can withstand a forty-million-dollar lawsuit from a billion-dollar corporation? How many of you have the extra cash around to pay for your defense, much less the extra time to defend yourself?" The academy started this fund to ensure that emergency doctors have the ability to speak their minds on issues of importance to the profession. It took two years for a judge to rule that the First Amendment protected Schwartz's opinion.[50]

Emergency physicians are not the only medical specialists to feel the sting of SLAPPs. Humana, Inc., filed a defamation suit against the chief of staff at its own hospital in Las Vegas. Dr. George M. Hemmeter had criticized Humana for not passing along discounts it received from its insurance operations to customers, as is required by law. He made his comments in a statement to the Nevada Senate Committee on Commerce and Labor in March 1989.[51] As in the case of other SLAPPs, Dr. Hemmeter was sued based on his communication to a government entity. But he SLAPPed back and was successful. At the trial of his counter-suit, Hemmeter fingered state insurance commissioners for covering up Humana's markups on ancillary services.[52] The jury awarded Hemmeter $9.8 million — $2.3 million in compensatory damages and $7.5 million in punitive damages.[53] Humana appealed but settled the case in 1994.[54]

Another SLAPP — filed by the Cancer Treatment Centers of America (CTCA), headquartered in Tulsa, Oklahoma, against four physicians who were critical of its operation in a *Dallas Morning News* article — caused more alarm bells to ring in the medical community. The four doctors were quoted in a story published in the newspaper. Yet the newspaper was not named in the lawsuit. The National Council Against Health Fraud commented on the lawsuit in its newsletter, saying, "The CTCA action appears to be a SLAPP suit . . . Of grave concern is the effect this action may have upon the willingness of experts to speak to the media. Reporters often complain that doctors and scientists are too closed-mouthed as it is. Although SLAPP suits are generally dismissed, they can be costly and time-consuming, making it easier to remain silent. Those of us who have seen the effect of anti-trust suits on the willingness of medical organizations to speak out on consumer issues have good reason for concern."[55]

The concern is a very real one. University of Denver sociologist Penelope Canan has found that people targeted by SLAPPs are less likely to participate in future public issues or discussions. Further, she learned that even the threat of a SLAPP suit can keep citizens from participating. What is more, people who merely know about SLAPPs are less likely to participate in public discourse than those who are not aware of this phenomenon.[56] When it comes to public discourse on medicine, Americans want their physicians to speak out, but doctors, like other citizens, can become reticent if it means a lengthy court battle and enormous legal fees.

A recent rash of lawsuits designed solely to intimidate or retaliate against citizens in the exercise of their First Amendment rights has been clearly identified and recognized by several courts and legislatures. Some citizens have paid thousands of dollars simply to defend a right guaranteed in the Constitution. Yet, the cost in terms of the public's participation in the democracy has been even greater. Studies show that SLAPP targets are reluctant to get involved in a community issue after facing the trauma of litigation. Consequently, the intimidation goal of filers is reached.

SLAPP suits cast a pall over the legitimate litigation rights of American business. From a practical standpoint, as courts and legislatures address the problems posed by SLAPPs, the filers will likely find themselves on the losing side of the legal equation. The public may fail to recognize the distinction between SLAPPs and legitimate claims for tortious interference with contract, and the resultant public sentiment may cloud judges' vision.

In sum, SLAPPs present a lose-lose scenario. Citizen-activists lose because they become disenfranchised from the democratic process by lawsuits, real or threatened. Harassment by litigation promises to hand businesses a double defeat — first, in terms of potential abuse of process damages and attorneys' fees, and second, in terms of a damaged corporate image.

3

Ivory Tower of Babel

"Several professors who cross the academic parameters of what may be said in the classroom have found themselves the object of organized vilification and administrative penalties."

— Dinesh D'Souza, *Illiberal Education*, 1991

On January 13, 1993, a group of African-American women students at the University of Pennsylvania passed the High Rise North residence hall on the Philadelphia campus. As they lingered outside the dormitory making noise and singing loudly for about twenty minutes, a freshman named Eden Jacobowitz opened the window of his sixth-floor room and shouted something that would ignite a nationwide controversy over racism and campus speech policies. The young man from Lawrence, Long Island, who was trying to write an English paper at the time, yelled, "Shut up, you water buffalo." He then told the women that if they were looking for a party, the zoo was a mile away. Jacobowitz was not the only student yelling that evening. By the time he joined in the fray, several other dorm residents had already begun shouting profanities at the group. Yet, when the police arrived, Eden Jacobowitz was the only one to admit to yelling out his dorm window that night. What followed was a whirlwind of events. He told the police that he had used the term "water buffalo," a literal translation from the Hebrew language for the word *behayma,* which is an epithet reserved for a crude individual. The women claimed the term was a racial epithet and thus violated Penn's speech code. They raised that issue before the university's Judicial Inquiry Office, but the university was forced to drop the charges against Jacobowitz after the women withdrew the complaint, saying the intense media coverage of the case would preclude them from receiving a fair hearing.

This incident is just one of many in the storm of controversy blanketing American colleges and universities. In the 1980s and early 1990s, universities became hotbeds of the phenomenon known as political correctness (PC). The PC movement garnered supporters among many students, faculty, and administrators, but the damage in terms of free speech is immeasurable. Students, faculty, and administrators are now often too fearful to speak their minds and risk ostracism, both blatant and subtle. When Chief Justice William H. Rehnquist told an audience gathered at the George Mason University commencement in 1993 that universities should expose students to the "marketplace of ideas" rather than suppress unpopular speech, he could not have chosen a better place — but he might have chosen a better time, such as freshman orientation. Although it seems a natural fit for the chief justice to address the newly graduated on the need for the free flow of expression, incoming freshmen (or "freshpersons," as the politically correct would have them called) could really use this message.

The need for early detection and prevention of censorship becomes evident in one of the more recent manifestations of PC — thefts of college newspapers carrying unpopular (or non-PC) views. Sometimes the papers are simply removed from campus. In other incidents, the pilferage takes on a more hostile tone. Such was the case at Penn State University, where copies of the *Lionhearted*, a conservative student newspaper, were set ablaze in front of the paper's financial backer's office. The four-year-old paper was first published in response to the perceived liberal bias of the established campus newspaper — the *Daily Collegian*. Adding to the fray in this college town was the decision by the area Knight-Ridder newspaper to reprint the *Lionhearted* free of charge.

The Knight-Ridder paper's response sent a strong message: The way to combat unpopular speech, no matter how sophomoric or hateful, is not by suppression. Rehnquist's speech to the George Mason University graduates struck a similar theme: "Ideas with which we disagree — so long as they remain ideas and not conduct which interferes with the rights of others — should be confronted with argument and persuasion, not suppression." Some critics like to draw a distinction between free speech and hate speech, but the law should not recognize the dichotomy. In *R.A.V. v. St. Paul*,[1] the Supreme Court observed that "the First Amendment does not permit . . . special prohibitions on those speakers who express views on disfavored subjects." The *St. Paul* case involved a cross burning on the residential property of a black family. Such expression was punished under a St. Paul ordinance. (The case is discussed fully in chapter five.)

What continues to be troubling is the number of educators who are quick to jump on the bandwagon of censorship simply because they do not approve of the message being conveyed. This attitude threatens to undermine the central mission of the university — to provide a broad education through a variety of viewpoints. According to Mark Goodman, executive director of the Student Press Law Center, in Washington, D.C., "censorship incidents on college campuses are on the increase." Goodman's work in helping to safeguard the student press has made him painfully aware that "there are many college administrators out there . . . that don't have a strong appreciation for the First Amendment and the values it's based on. As a result, when free expression becomes inconvenient or press freedom becomes inconvenient, they take steps to deal with it. The Constitution be damned."

Goodman has found that this lack of appreciation extends beyond administrators to other faculty members and even to students, although the administration has the ability to set the tone. "What we've seen in places where administrators have very strongly voiced their support for free expression and made clear they wouldn't tolerate efforts by others to limit it, that's usually the most significant impact on what happens and the efforts to censor eventually dwindle."

Goodman says calls to the Student Press Law Center have increased by about 100 percent in the past five years, giving him the feeling that the situation on campuses is worsening. Goodman is careful to not sound too cynical, but he says he "definitely thinks the pendulum is swinging away from the notion of freedom right now."

CAMPUS DWELLERS MUST KNOW THE CODE

Some colleges and universities have gone so far as to codify restrictions on speech. The rationale behind speech codes is actually quite laudable; the result is what erodes constitutional life on college campuses. Administrators have long felt the need to create an environment that is tolerant of all peoples from other cultures. Naturally, universities did not feel compelled to tolerate bigotry. But soon enough speech not comporting to the politically correct view of the way things ought to be was labeled racist and was punished. Accordingly, what started out as a good idea developed into a nightmarish ordeal for many students and faculty. The recent history of race relations on campus is critical to a fuller understanding of the development of speech codes.

Many of our nation's college campuses are located in remote areas. Some, in fact, are far removed from urban areas where large populations of people of diverse cultures typically live. In such a remote location, the college or university is the only vehicle through which diversity is introduced into the communities surrounding the campus. The influx of minority populations is not always welcomed. Most of the individuals who staff the university, though not typically the faculty, were born and reared in those communities. Consequently, the hometown people did not grow up in an environment in which they were exposed to people of other cultures.

On the other side of the equation, recruiting minority students and faculty to these remote areas is troublesome. The students do not often feel comfortable in an environment where there are few others like themselves. Minority faculty and staff feel the sting of solitude even more, for the students can look forward to graduation and a return to the area of their choice, but faculty and staff members presumably want to carve out a career and must contemplate spending several years in one location.

The problems start to develop in a cyclical fashion. To make coming to the particular college or university attractive to minority students and faculty, the administration must sweeten the deal. The supply of minority faculty across the country is still extremely low in light of the demand. Universities must fashion offers based on this market demand, which typically means higher salaries and other perks. Minority faculty are sometimes given reduced course loads to teach or higher research stipends. As for the students being recruited, they are often given scholarships, spending money, special program options, and minority advisers who provide extra attention to them.

Because other colleges and universities are doing the same things, the competition to attract minorities is stiff. A vicious cycle develops because majority students, faculty, and staff become envious of the special perks received by their minority counterparts. That jealousy often turns to anger, and thus tensions develop between majority and minority populations. Academic institutions are among the worst at handling these situations, and administrators who feel the solution to attracting minorities, both students and faculty or staff, is to throw money at them only fuel the problem. Moreover, administrators often manifest the attitude that the majority population has to accept what they are doing without question. Student, faculty, or staff members who raise even legitimate questions about the special treatment sometimes face sanctions.

Over the past decade, people who make their living on college and university campuses have learned to keep their mouths shut if they wish to avoid problems. Further exacerbating their anger is the fact that most campuses have faced great budget crunches over the past few years. Programs and positions have been cut. Yet, despite some critical budget cutbacks, many campuses have refused to cut funding to minority programs because of their commitment to bring more cultural diversity to their environs or for fear of the political backlash associated with cutting such programs.

The culture of fear to express oneself has grown exponentially with the creation of speech codes on campuses. These regulations, promulgated in the name of tolerance, punish a variety of expression ranging from racial epithets to "inappropriate laughter." They typically punish expression that insults or stigmatizes an individual or group based on sex, race, ethnic origin, or sexual orientation. In 1994, the Freedom Forum First Amendment Center released a study titled *War of Words: Speech Codes at Public*

71

Colleges and Universities. The focus of the report was on public, rather than private, institutions because public colleges and universities must adhere to the First Amendment. In other words, public institutions are government actors for First Amendment purposes.

The report found that more than 380 colleges and universities have some type of speech regulations. The study looked at the arguments both for and against speech codes and culled the common themes. The report was updated in 1995 and concluded that many campuses, concerned about hate speech, are thinking twice about inviting speakers such as Louis Farrakhan or G. Gordon Liddy.

VICTIMS OF SPEECH

Advocates of speech codes typically treat minorities as victims. Some legal scholars have made much of the "victims" theory of jurisprudence. This theory focuses on the effects of speech on those targeted by the message or racial epithet and their relative inability to respond under traditional First Amendment. To this end, Professor Mari J. Matsuda, of the University of Hawaii's School of Law, has argued that the law should provide these "victims" with a special category. She wrote:

The places where the law does not go to redress harm have tended to be places where women, children, people of color and poor people live. This absence of law is itself another story with a message, perhaps unintended, about the relative value of different human lives. A legal response to racist speech is a statement that victims of racism are valued members of our polity.[2]

Although Professor Matsuda's ideas are well intentioned and have been accepted by some on the nation's campuses, they also cast aside hard-fought challenges that strengthened the First Amendment over the decades — and they threaten to undermine the protections of speech that aid us all, including the class of "victims" she describes. Matsuda bases her thesis on a number of anecdotes of egregious intolerance, and she dismisses the long-held maxim that the answer to irrational speech is rational speech. In fact, she believes that tolerance of racist remarks by those in authority is as hurtful to the recipient as the remarks themselves. Rather, her argument calls for an appeal to humanity: "However irrational racist speech may be, it hits right at the emotional place where we feel the most pain."[3] She has developed a test to determine if the particular speech in question is racist hate speech. It has three prongs. First, the message is of racial inferiority; second, the message is directed against a historically oppressed group; and third, the message is persecutorial, hateful, and degrading.[4] Matsuda would not only tolerate but encourage restrictions on such speech — a classic content-driven prohibition. But under her analysis, these "victims" could hurl hateful epithets at over-represented groups with impunity.

Her argument begins to break down when faced with the situation of one "oppressed" group's directing hateful messages at another. She recognizes that the so-called victim's privilege is "problematic." "While I have argued . . . for tolerance of hateful speech that comes from an experience of oppression, when that speech is used to attack a subordinated group member, using language of persecution, and adopting a rhetoric of racial inferiority, I am inclined to prohibit such speech," she says.[5] Keeping Matsuda's views straight would send the courts into a tailspin and defy a logical legal analysis.

Professor Rhonda G. Hartman, a visiting law professor at the University of Pittsburgh who believes that good speech will not counteract the bad, explored the notion by analogizing hate speech to other categories of nonprotected speech. She observed that "fighting words" (remarks that tend to drive the person addressed to violent acts), "incitement of illegal acts," and "obscenity" all share basic features. First, "each category consists only of speech that threatens serious harm to some public interest."[6] Second, "each category includes only speech that bypasses the rational, evaluative capacity of its hearer in some way."[7] Hartman observed that counterspeech (the solution often offered by opponents of speech codes) will not work. She concluded that by preempting further speech, rather than inviting response, hate speech on campus "undercuts First Amendment values" and thus is less deserving of protection.[8]

Ironically, the same argument can be used as support for abandoning all speech codes on college and university campuses. Speech codes and the orthodoxy surrounding them can be shown to preempt further speech. As First Amendment commentator, columnist, and author Nat Hentoff wrote in his aptly titled book *Free Speech for Me — But Not for Thee*:

> One brave student at New York University Law School, Barry Endick, actually signed his name a few years ago to a complaint about this bristling orthodoxy in a letter in the law school student publication, the *Commentator*. He told of the atmosphere in the law school created by a "host of watchdog committees and a generally hostile classroom reception regarding any student right of center." This "can be arguably viewed as symptomatic of a prevailing spirit of academic and social tolerance of . . . any idea which is not 'politically correct' . . . we ought to examine why students, so anxious to wield the Fourteenth Amendment [equal protection] give short shrift to the First."[9]

Hentoff quoted another student's lament: "A lot of times I don't want to speak up in class. Otherwise, I'd have forty percent of the class on me saying I'm a counterrevolutionary racist fascist."[10] Still another student told of an " 'unwritten suspension of free speech,' but will not challenge it. 'I want to blend in with the community. And nothing I could say would do any good anyhow.' "[11]

These examples reveal that the real victim of restrictions on campus speech is the educational process. The process that once called for free and open discussion has now been cloaked in suppression — and students now fear to address sensitive areas. Speech codes that contribute to this atmosphere of fear are undermining classroom discussion — the bedrock of the learning process. Anyone who has ever been in a classroom as either a student or a teacher can attest to the staleness that takes place if students are unwilling to give of themselves in the classroom setting. Lecture without interaction is not only tedious but unrewarding in terms of engaged learning. And because more and more educators are placing the emphasis on *learning* rather than on teaching, it should be apparent that students learn when they become engaged in the process. Unfortunately, the climate of fear being cultivated on so many campuses by the politically correct drives a wedge into that important process.

Willingness to participate in learning is almost

instinctual. To test this thesis, simply visit any kindergarten classroom in America. These five- and six-year-olds cannot get their hands high enough in the air to volunteer responses to the teacher's questions. They often become so overcome by their own enthusiasm that they have to be gently reminded of the convention of waiting to be acknowledged before offering their answers. These youngsters are blithely unaware that someone else might view their responses as offensive. How sad that when these students attend college, armed with the knowledge that the document that laid the foundation for the nation protects their participation, they feel unable to state their views.

THE COURTS "DECODE" THE CAMPUS

In the handful of speech code cases that have been challenged in the courts, the First Amendment has prevailed because courts have viewed rules as content-based restrictions. In constitutional analysis, courts make an important distinction between regulations that punish people for the content of the message and those that merely impose restrictions on the time, place, or manner of the speech and remain neutral with respect to the content of the message. For example, a city ordinance that prohibits the distribution of political literature is content-specific. It specifies a prohibition on a particular

77

content of speech; that is, *political* literature. On the other hand, an ordinance that prohibits the use of sound trucks in residential neighborhoods between the hours of eight P.M. and six A.M. does so without concern for the content of the message to be broadcast. The latter has an easier time passing constitutional muster, as long as the city can show a substantial or important reason for having the ordinance and that alternate channels of communications exist.

For content-specific regulations to be permissible, the city in the above illustration must demonstrate that a compelling interest exists and that it has used the least-restrictive means for accomplishing that interest. In other words, courts must apply the highest or strictest level of scrutiny. At the University of Wisconsin, for example, the board of regents had adopted a code titled "Policy and Guidelines on Racist and Discriminatory Conduct." The board had received help from a group of law professors who believed the code would pass constitutional muster "if it included a requirement that the speaker intended to make the educational environment hostile for the individual being addressed." To this end the rule defined the offenses accordingly:

The University may discipline a student in non-academic matters in the following situations:

(2)(a) For racist or discriminatory comments, epithets or other expressive behavior directed at an individual or on separate occasions at different individuals, or for physical conduct, if such comments, epithets or other expressive behavior or physical conduct intentionally —

1. demean the race, sex, religion, color, creed, disability, sexual orientation, national origin, ancestry or age of the individual or individuals; and

2. create an intimidating, hostile or demeaning environment for education, University-related work, or other University-authorized activity.[12]

By the time the case reached the federal court for the Eastern District of Wisconsin, nine students had been sanctioned for speech violations ranging from calling another student a "shaka-zulu" to calling another a "fucking bitch."[13] When the university sought to lump the code under the First Amendment exception for "fighting words" (see chapter five), the court balked, saying, "Since the elements of the UW rule do not require that the regulated speech, by its very utterance, tend to incite violent reaction, the rule goes beyond the scope of the fighting words doctrine."[14] Although attempts by proponents to meld such speech codes into recognized First Amendment exceptions is understandable, it is illogical for the law to view these codes as anything other than what they are — content-based restrictions on speech subject to the highest level of judicial scrutiny. Moreover, because these codes are written to encompass a wide variety of infractions and give sanctioning authorities the widest latitude for enforcement, the codes are often overbroad, or at a minimum, not the least-prohibitive approach to achieving the university's interest.

The overbreadth doctrine of constitutional law is a useful tool in helping to preserve the safeguards of the First Amendment. If a rule designed to regulate speech that is regulable (e.g., fighting words) is so broad that it also restricts permissible speech (e.g., inflamed rhetoric that does not rise to the level required of the fighting words doctrine), then the rule should be declared unconstitutional. In other words, government cannot include protected speech in the mix when it seeks to proscribe unprotected speech. Another related doctrine requires a court to strike down provisions that are "vague." If people cannot discern what speech is being prohibited by reading the regulation, it cannot pass constitutional muster.

Like officials at Wisconsin, University of Michigan administrators found a "rising tide of racial intolerance and harassment on campus"[15] and sought to legitimize a speech code there on that basis. The Michigan code prohibited verbal or physical behavior "that stigmatizes or victimizes an individual on the basis of race, ethnicity, religion, sex, sexual orientation, creed, national origin, ancestry, age, marital status, handicap or Vietnam-era veteran status . . ."[16] The purpose of the code was to create a tolerant environment on campus, but as the court explained, "The policy swept within its scope a significant amount of 'verbal conduct' or 'verbal behavior' which is unquestionably protected speech under the First Amendment."[17]

The court was also mindful of an "interpretive guide" that was published by the university's Affirmative Action Office shortly after the policy was adopted. The guide provided some examples of the types of infractions covered by the policy. These included: "A flyer containing racist threats distributed in a residence hall; Racist graffiti written on the door of an Asian student's study carrel; A male student makes a remark in class like 'Women just aren't as good in this field as men,' thus creating a hostile learning environment for female classmates; Students in a residence hall have a floor party and invite everyone on their floor except one person because they think she might be a lesbian; A black student is confronted and racially insulted by two white students in a cafeteria; Male students leave pornographic pictures and jokes on the desk of a female graduate student; Two men demand that their roommate in the residence hall move out and be tested for AIDS."[18]

If these were not sufficient examples to illustrate the point, the guide also pronounced that a student was a "harasser" when ... "You exclude someone from a study group because that person is of a different race, sex, or ethnic origin than you are; You tell jokes about gay men and lesbians; Your student organization sponsors entertainment that includes a comedian who slurs Hispanics; You display a confederate flag on the door of your room in the residence hall; You laugh at a joke about someone in your class who stutters; You make obscene telephone calls or send racist notes or computer messages; You comment in a derogatory way about a particular person's or group's physical appearance or sexual orientation, or their cultural origins, or religious beliefs."

It is no wonder students on campuses today are fearful of contributing to a discussion. Thankfully, the federal courts struck down Michigan's and Wisconsin's codes. Of course, these decisions did not stop officials at both schools from attempting to refine the codes to meet objections. It is unfortunate that university officials wish to expend so much time and effort trying to get around the First Amendment rather than simply embracing it. If, as in one of the examples listed above, a student says that women do not belong in a particular field, the best response to such an outrageous statement is not to punish the student but rather to prove him wrong with specific examples refuting his theorem — in other words, to counter his speech with facts showing him the illogic of his premise. That can only be accomplished with more speech. The University of Michigan's response — punishing the student for making such a statement in the first place — does nothing to help educate that student. If anything it simply feeds into his notion that the university views women as victims and must step in and protect them by punishing him.

In *Doe v. University of Michigan*, the court concluded with a reference to speech codes at private institutions "not subject to the strictures of the First Amendment."[19] In order to have a First Amendment infringement, there must be some action by government (including state-operated colleges and universities). The court quoted Yale historian C. Vann Woodward, who represented a student charged with "disseminating a malicious flyer intended to ridicule the homosexual community." In a *New York Times* article, Woodward wrote:

It simply seems unnatural to make a fuss about the rights of a speaker who offends the moral or political convictions passionately held by a majority. The far more natural impulse is to stop the nonsense, shut it up, punish it — anything but defend it. But to give rein to that inclination would be to make the majority the arbiters of truth for all. Furthermore, it would put universities into the business of censorship.[20]

Professor Woodward is correct. These codes thrust university officials into the role of censor — a role too many of them are now more than willing to accept. This is also sufficient reason to abandon the codes. At Tufts and the University of Pennsylvania (both private institutions), the codes were rescinded after the universities themselves concluded that "they were ineffectual, divisive or illegal."[21] The wake-up call came at Penn after the Jacobowitz incident made national headlines. In abolishing Penn's speech code, Interim President Claire Fagin and Interim Provost Marvin Lazerson issued a joint statement, saying, "We cannot depend upon the enforcement of the policy to achieve a community dedicated to the free exchange of ideas and the protection of its members from harassment and abuse."[22] As a postscript, Eden Jacobowitz contends that his life at the University of Pennsylvania was a living hell in the time the code was in effect and charges were pending against him, and in February 1996, he filed a lawsuit against the university seeking $50,000 in damages for infliction of emotional distress. The case has been settled.

Dinesh D'Souza, a research fellow at the American Enterprise Institute, studied the effects of political correctness on campus. The results of his research were published in a 1991 book, *Illiberal Education: The Politics of Race and*

Sex on Campus. Since his research in the late 1980s and early 1990s, D'Souza says he spends about half of his time lecturing on college campuses and keeps attuned of events. Even more than explicit enactments regulating speech, what D'Souza now sees is the result of an "intolerant political culture" or "what John Stuart Mill had in mind when he said that one of the most profound forms of tyranny is not the explicit legal enactment but a kind of social pressure that excommunicates an unpopular point of view." People whose views are in opposition to the politically correct's "are stigmatized or driven from the field with accusations and epithets."

The "trump card" in the debate about diversity and multiculturalism is racism, according to D'Souza. "Not only the charge of racism, but the fear of being called a racist in some form, has an inhibiting effect in discussing a whole range of issues." Students, faculty, staff, and administrators will consciously avoid subjects for fear of creating an uncomfortable situation for themselves — one that might indeed snowball into a career-ender. "In that sense, the accusation of racism becomes a tool of censorship — censorship used in the loose sense of discouraging and driving from the public square ideas and arguments," D'Souza said.

The irony of all this cannot be lost in the discussion. D'Souza views it in a liberal-conservative model: "The irony is that liberalism in its

85

campaign against intolerance is able to make a major exception for itself." He found that conservatives are more cynical; they laugh at the situation and "life's craziness." On the other hand, "the animating liberal emotion is indignation — 'that's an outrage; this is unjust; this can't be' — while, in a moral sense, [this] is healthy because it springs from idealism, it is much more closely wedded to intolerance because the indignation supplies the moral justification for shutting the other guy up."

The debate, however, cannot and should not be viewed just in terms of the liberal-conservative ideology. Many from both camps have felt the sting of the undercurrent of censorship. The First Amendment is an odd political animal in this way because its supporters come from both sides of the political spectrum. Even a conservative icon such as Justice Antonin Scalia voted with the majority in striking down flag desecration laws as unconstitutional (see chapter five). Burning the flag is considered symbolic speech. Destroying the message itself has become more popular in college and university settings.

As the Student Press Law Center's Mark Goodman sees it, "no matter how well intentioned, it is impossible to draw something narrowly enough not to silence legitimate expression at the same time you're silencing behavior that is illegitimate." The other factor for Goodman, independent of the ability to enforce the code, is that free speech is so fundamental to the notion of academic inquiry and learning that it must be accepted that offensive, hurtful expression is inevitable, just as it is in our democratic society. "Speech codes silence or limit debate on issues that are very important," he said.

GROUP THINK

Dan Loccarini was tired of all the good press homosexuals were getting. That is what prompted him to launch a new student organization at Penn State University called STRAIGHT, an acronym for STudents Reinforcing Adherence in General Heterosexual Tradition. But when he tried to get a charter as a student organization, he was turned down by the student government's supreme court. To be chartered as a student organization, a group had to meet three criteria: (1) it had to have a unique purpose; (2) it had to have at least twelve members; and (3) it must better the university. The student court found that the group met only the first two criteria. The members of the court did not believe such a group bettered the university. The problem with the decision was that the university, through its students, was singling out a particular group it found distasteful based on its message. Other groups on campus could be considered offensive to some people but had been chartered nonetheless.

Loccarini and his group's members could also interject the First Amendment into the mix because Penn State is a state-related university. Accordingly, for First Amendment purposes, the university is considered a government actor because it receives a portion of its funding from the state. This funding supplies the needed connection to government required to raise First Amendment arguments. The denial of the charter to STRAIGHT appeared on the surface to be viewpoint-based discrimination. In other words, the reason these students could not get a charter, which would enable them to apply for student activities funding and hold meetings in university buildings, was that the student government did not like the group's antigay views. Members of the Lesbian, Gay, and Bisexual Student Alliance feared the group would promote violence against its members, although Loccarini denied that was a mission for the group.

STRAIGHT appealed the decision, and in March 1997, an appeals board granted a charter to the organization. Now STRAIGHT is a recognized student group at Penn State. It may use the university letterhead and can share the more than $1 million of funding that is parceled out to the university's student groups. It may not, however, discriminate, and thus lesbians, gays, and bisexuals are free to join.

AN ARTFUL DODGE

In spring 1997, Penn State was the site of another First Amendment controversy that put the university in the news. This time the subject was artistic expression. When the work of art student Christine Enedy went on display in one of the campus galleries, it drew both the attention and the ire of some religious groups on campus. Her work was titled "25 Years of Virginity: A Self-Portrait," and it included twenty-five pairs of underwear with a cross sewn into the crotch of each. As the story made its way into the news, some state legislators became miffed at the display. The story broke just at the time Penn State's president had to make his way to Harrisburg for funding hearings before the state appropriations committee. As is often the case in such instances, the lawmakers directed some heat his way.

Penn State's president, Graham B. Spanier, defended the university's position of not censoring students' work. He later told the university community, "There must be some fundamental principles by which we stand. I can't envision any circumstance under which this university would want to encourage censorship."[23] Spanier backed the School of Visual Art's policy of sensitizing students in its programs about the public feelings their work might arouse. Faculty and students there must discuss these issues before a work is displayed. Enedy's art remained on display in the campus gallery.

This incident at Penn State is important in terms of the public pressure that can be placed on universities in tight budget times. While defending the First Amendment has its own psychic value, administrators at public universities must please a number of constituencies, not all of which are on campus. People in the communities surrounding the campus as well as state legislators who vote on funding allocations feel entitled to weigh in on campus controversies. Many of those constituents strongly advocate censorship of material that offends them. This often places colleges and universities in uncomfortable, if not untenable, circumstances.

DESTROYING UNPOPULAR SPEECH

When 6000 copies of the *Lionhearted*, a conservative newspaper at Penn State University disappeared on April 20, 1993, some might have initially thought the incident to be a college prank. When a bundle of them appeared in flames on the lawn of a university trustee who sponsored the publication, most knew it was much more than that. The *Lionhearted* was started by a conservative cohort in response to what they perceived as the liberal bias of the independent school newspaper, the *Daily Colle-*

gian. The trustee whose lawn was chosen as the site of the immolation had provided the initial financial backing for the upstart periodical.

A favorite target of the new newspaper was Penn State's Women's Studies Program. In the pilfered edition, a caricature appeared depicting a female *Collegian* columnist in a scant bikini sitting on a bed with a sign above her that read FEMINIST AT WORK. After a brief investigation, police arrested two women, both students at the university and both journalism majors, in the theft. The arrests touched off a flurry of controversy on the campus and in the community, and as a result the district attorney granted essentially probation without verdict under a first-offender program. He vowed, however, that he would not be so lenient the next time. Several thefts of the newspaper occurred thereafter, albeit in smaller numbers, but no one was charged. The paper eventually ceased publication, ostensibly proving to its detractors that marketplace forces work.

Part of the controversy around the incident arose when some members of Penn State's faculty voiced public approval of the theft. Two days after the incident, a Women's Studies faculty member, citing the venomous content of the *Lionhearted*, said, "It's not free speech, it's hate speech."[24] She also believed that the entire issue was being cast inappropriately: "The point has been protest, but it has been framed as censorship. No reporter wants to talk about the content of the paper. It's men wanting to hide the issue. Men can always hide behind the First Amendment."[25] The Penn State incident was not an isolated one. The Student Press Law Center has tracked numerous incidents of newspaper vandalism and theft across the country.

SPLC's Mark Goodman said he fears stealing newspapers as a form of protest is going to become routine. "In a period of two years, we've gone from five or six newspaper theft incidents in an entire school year to twenty-five or thirty newspaper theft incidents in a school year." People are using newspaper thefts to express dissatisfaction with the campus newspapers, and unfortunately it has become an accepted tactic. Goodman attributes this attitude to administrators who have refused to stand against it. Goodman's tracking of these incidents shows that a high percentage of the thefts is related to "PC concerns — objections that the publication is racist or sexist or homophobic or defensive at least to one of those groups."

The trend continued in the 1995–96 academic year. Twenty-six incidents of newspaper theft were reported to the Student Press Law Center.[26] The SPLC reported that more and more thefts were related to race relations on campus. One such racial incident occurred on the Birmingham campus of the University of Alabama in the previous academic year and resulted in the theft of 5,500 copies of the campus newspaper, the *Kaleidoscope*.

On June 14, 1994, the *Kaleidoscope* disappeared from every outdoor newspaper rack on campus on the Alabama campus within two hours of its distribution. A caller to the newspaper reported that Chinese students were removing the papers. These students were upset over articles about a professor who had been arrested. According to *Kaleidoscope* adviser Stephen Chappel, "the student staff on the paper had been covering for about six months a story that unfolded when a researcher in our medical end of campus had been accused of raping three of his graduate assistants." All of the people involved in the incident — the three students and the professor — were from China and were in the United States on visas. The professor was dismissed from the university and was convicted. The students then filed a civil suit against the professor. His conviction was overturned on appeal.

The week prior to the appellate court's decision a summary judgment was entered against him in the civil action. The campus newspaper ran a story about the case. "We received a phone call from a student, who identified himself as a Chinese male, who said the story did not belong in the paper because what the professor had done was not wrong in Chinese culture. Chinese females don't have rights, and if he wants to have sexual relations with them, that's fine," Chappel said. The caller informed the newspaper that Chinese students had taken the newspapers.

The following week, when another story was published about the case, some two thousand copies of the newspaper were stolen. "At that point the Chinese community said the newspaper was making things bad for them," Chappel reported.

These incidents were just the beginning of trouble for the newspaper. The campus police were uncooperative. The chief told the student editor of the paper when he reported the theft, "You can't steal something that is free. It's not a crime." The vice president for administration was a bit more concerned about the incident but not enough to really push the issue. The local prosecutor also believed that free publications cannot be "stolen." Chappel learned a lesson from the incident: "Now we have a disclaimer on the editorial page that says the first copy is free. Additional copies are twenty-five cents. We also put that disclaimer on our racks that are around campus."

Gordon "Mac" McKerral, the campus newspaper adviser at Troy State University, had to do the same thing there. This disclaimer followed an incident in which a student arrested in connection with the theft of a credit card stole bundles of the paper that detailed his alleged crimes. McKerral was required to break down the per-paper production and circulation costs in order to convince the district attorney that the free paper had value. McKerral sought retribution for the theft because he feared this shutting off of information was becoming too common: "It's happening all over the country for one reason or another. Fraternities grab them when they're going to get dinged by a story. People take them because they don't like editorial policy. It really doesn't matter what the impetus is. It's just wrong to do this and it's becoming too frequent."

Punishment for speech on campus is becoming an all too frequent occurrence. Censorship of speech in this environment should be considered not just wrongheaded but wrong. Institutions of higher learning must be places where ideas can be vigorously debated. Unfortunately, many colleges and universities have replaced an atmosphere that celebrates robust debate with a culture of suppression. Forcing racism underground does not make it go away. In most cases, sunlight is the best disinfectant.

4

Television and the Courts

"Without the ability to witness the actual proceedings on television, many Americans could be left only with the sensationalist distillations of the supermarket tabloids."

— *New York Times* editorial, 1994

The People of California v. Orenthal James Simpson — the so-called trial of the century — captured the attention of the American public for more than a year. Beginning with a televised chase scene on a Los Angeles freeway, this "made-for-television" case made icons out of bloody gloves and posturing celebrity attorneys. It also led to a spate of books, television interviews, new celebrities, and renewed interest in the role cameras play in the American courtroom. The Simpson case has also spurred some major reflection about the relationship between the media and the courts. Although this case handily wins the "camera-courtroom" word association game, other televised trials in this decade provide a more pristine example of how the First Amendment's right of a free press jibes with the Sixth Amendment's guarantee of a fair trial for the criminally accused.

The topic of cameras in the courtroom continues to be hotly debated. Opponents of televised trials believe a defendant's right to a fair trial by an impartial panel of peers is jeopardized when lawyers, witnesses, jurors, and judges are under the scrutiny of a television audience. The O. J. Simpson trial elevated the debate to a new level, and questions remain as to what effect the case will have on televised access to trials. The National Center for State Courts reports that forty-seven states permit cameras in their courtrooms.[1] This figure takes into account any permissible access, but states clearly vary with respect to how much coverage is allowed. For instance, Pennsylvania is counted among the states allowing cameras, but the state's Code of Judicial Conduct provides for television only in civil, nonjury proceedings in which the judge, all parties, and each witness who will appear agree to the coverage. This canon gives little opportunity to the news media, especially because criminal (the more newsworthy) proceedings are completely excluded.

The federal courts, on the other hand, have been closed to TV cameras for most of their history. In 1991, the federal Judicial Conference authorized a three-year experiment in which six United States District Courts and two Courts of

Appeal allowed televised coverage of civil cases. Despite a favorable response by the judges involved, the conference discontinued coverage after the three-year period. The decision not to continue the experiment came down in September 1994 — after the televised preliminary hearing in the Simpson case. In 1995, a group of federal judges urged the conference to reconsider its decision. The result of that reconsideration was a March 1996 ruling that allows cameras and recording equipment in the appellate circuits, but trial courts — typically the more newsworthy venues — remain closed. Despite this latest move, media coverage of civil cases, particularly at the appellate level, will undoubtedly be scant. Bruce Collins, vice president and general counsel of C-SPAN, the national cable network devoted to public affairs programming, who also chaired the American Bar Association's committee on media-bar relations, observed that "the media aren't going to cover court proceedings simply because a local court is part of the experiment. It has to have a story that the media think is worthy of attention."

WHERE THE ACTION IS

The states friendly to television cameras in their courts provided the impetus for the media-savvy legal publisher Steven Brill to launch in 1991 a twenty-four-hour cable network devoted exclusively to trials and coverage of the legal system. Brill's Court TV came at a time when other organizations were considering such ventures, but his experience in legal media went unmatched. It also came on the heels of the tenth anniversary of CNN, the twenty-four-hour cable news operation that had experienced global success in the preceding decade. CNN had also captured an audience with its coverage of the 1984 New Bedford, Massachusetts, rape trial in which six Portuguese immigrants stood charged with a gang rape on a barroom pool table of a twenty-two-year-old woman. The CNN experience was an indication of the public's taste for coverage of the judicial system.

Although CNN had twenty-four hours to fill, gavel-to-gavel courtroom coverage still presented a risk for the fledgling network. Several points needed to be factored into such a programming decision, according to CNN's executive vice president, Bob Furnad. "The first consideration is what is the potential news that's going to come out of the event. What is its newsworthiness, its news value? The secondary consideration is: Is it very elitist and going to be of such minute appeal that it doesn't serve the network well to put it on?" The ratings for CNN's court coverage have proved that it was a sound programming decision. Court TV reports that it applies similar criteria:

Court TV weighs several factors when choosing which trials to air, including how important and interesting the issues in the case are, the notoriety and newsworthy nature of both the case and the people involved, the quality of the "story," its educational value, and the expected duration of the trial. To ensure there is no bias for covering trials based solely on how popular they are, Court TV declines all requests to release the ratings of a specific trial, and its production staff is never privy to that information.[2]

CNN and Court TV got a boost in their courtroom coverage when William Kennedy Smith came to trial in December 1991 for rape; both organizations carried the proceedings live. Yet CNN's Furnad insists that the case did not start out as a litmus test for further coverage: "I don't think we went into it thinking that this will tell us a lot about whether we should be doing it or not. I think once we got into it and saw the public's acceptance of it, then, that said, this is something not to forget. In the same way, if we had taken it and we had done point-ones for ten days, we would have said this is something that we're not going to do again unless it's an incredibly important trial." The ratings, however, were far from a point-one. During the Simpson case, CNN increased its daily audience size fivefold during the live testimony, and during the testimony of some critical witnesses that figure soared to ten times its regular size.

Ratings often shape the criticism of courtroom coverage. Critics contend that television coverage is a form of electronic voyeurism — only the provocative cases attracting large audiences will ever be aired. If this is true in any fashion, Court TV maintains that the attraction is not generated by the coverage itself. "And while important trials may involve an element of 'entertainment,' this is not a new phenomenon or one related to television. In 1965, legal studies cited by the Supreme Court noted: 'In early frontier America, when no motion pictures, no television, and no radio provided entertainment, trial day in the county was like fair day, and from near and far, citizens young and old converged on the county seat. The criminal trial was the theatre and spectaculum of old rural America.' "[3] Clearly, the public's interest in criminal trials did not come of age with the growth of television. Moreover, television coverage presents only part of the picture about the struggle between the media's newsgathering process and the rights of the criminally accused. In fact, much of the public's angst with the camera in court may be misdirected. The real crux of disgust may be the publicity surrounding the trial. That subject is hardly a new one. One celebrated case from the 1950s — a case that took twelve years to resolve — helps to illustrate the other part of the story.

A MEDIA CIRCUS — BEFORE
TELEVISION'S HEYDAY

Four decades before O.J. became part of the daily diet, another murder trial captured the attention of the American public despite the lack of live television coverage. It was, however, similarly marked by a "carnival atmosphere" and led to a sweeping reform of the relationship between the media and the courts. The case was *The State of Ohio v. Samuel H. Sheppard*, and it set the tenor by which television coverage cautiously flows.

According to Dr. Sam Sheppard, his pregnant wife, Marilyn, was asleep in her bedroom on the night of July 4, 1954. Sheppard had fallen asleep on the downstairs couch while watching television. He awoke to his wife's screams and ran upstairs to investigate. When he reached her he saw what he described as a "form" standing over his wife's bed. He struggled with the form before being knocked unconscious. Upon coming to, he found his wife brutally murdered. Sheppard then heard a noise downstairs, investigated, and pursued the assailant to the lakeshore, where he once again struggled and lost consciousness.[4]

What happened next was a whirlwind criminal investigation and pressure by the media to focus on Sam Sheppard as the prime suspect. Hundreds of articles appeared in the Cleveland area media — 399 in the *Cleveland Press* alone.[5] Representative of the stories were two published in the *Press*. On July 20, 1954, the headline read SOMEONE IS GETTING AWAY WITH MURDER. What followed was a front-page editorial calling for the arrest of Dr. Sam Sheppard. Ten days later the *Press* carried another editorial (again on the front page), headlined WHY ISN'T SAM SHEPPARD IN JAIL? Before that day was over Sam Sheppard was in police custody, charged with the murder of his wife. Even before his arrest Sam Sheppard was found guilty of the crime by County Coroner Samuel R. Gerber, an ambitious career politician wielding great power in Cuyahoga County, Ohio. He concluded his autopsy report on Marilyn Sheppard with a verdict: "I further find that the injuries that caused this death were inflicted by her husband, Dr. Samuel H. Sheppard, and that death was homicidal in nature."[6]

Much pressure was placed on the coroner to conduct an inquest into Marilyn Sheppard's death. In fact, the *Cleveland Press* ran another frontpage editorial on July 21, 1954, with the headline WHY NO INQUEST? DO IT NOW, DR. GERBER.[7] A McCarthy-style hearing followed, with Gerber questioning the witnesses. Although the media were allowed in with obtrusive cameras clicking, Sheppard's attorney was removed for having "repeatedly interrupted the process of this trial." Less than three weeks after he was taken into custody, Sheppard was indicted by a grand jury whose foreman claimed he was under enormous pressure, including pressure from the media blanketing the area with stories. By the time jury selection began in October, the national (and even international) media had become absorbed with the case — with reporters filling most of the seats in the courtroom.

The publicity became so widespread that a continuance of the case was requested (it was denied). Radio stations began to set up remote equipment at the courthouse, and regular programs about the case were aired, including a debate about whether Sheppard was guilty based on the fact that he had hired a well-known criminal lawyer. The fledgling television industry also seized the opportunity to put "true crime" on the air. Celebrity journalists, including Dorothy Kilgallen and Walter Winchell, reported on the case. A dozen years later, when the United States Supreme Court finally decided the case, its opinion characterized the widespread attention this way:

> For months the virulent publicity about Sheppard and the murder had made the case notorious. Charges and countercharges were aired in the news media besides those for which Sheppard was called to trial. In addition, only three months before trial, Sheppard was examined for more than five hours

without counsel during a three-day inquest which ended in a public brawl. The inquest was televised live from a high school gymnasium seating hundreds of people. Furthermore, the trial began two weeks before a hotly contested election at which both Chief Prosecutor Mahon and Judge Blythin were candidates for judgeships.[8]

With all its shortcomings, the trial ended four days before Christmas in 1954 with a conviction of second-degree murder.

SHEPPARD V. MAXWELL:
JUSTICE REVISITED

Sam Sheppard went to jail, and it was twelve years before his conviction was finally reversed. The case went through the appeals process in Ohio and eventually to the United States Supreme Court, which declined to look at the case the first time it was presented with the opportunity. A decade after the original trial ended, Sam Sheppard was released from prison after a federal judge was convinced by Sheppard's new lawyer, F. Lee Bailey, that he had been denied a fair trial. After this, the U.S. Supreme Court decided to revisit the case.

The main thrust of Sheppard's argument (written by Bailey) to the Supreme Court was that extensive prejudicial publicity had made it impossible for him to get a fair trial. His brief set out numerous examples of the media frenzy engulfing the case. In fact, an appendix to the brief included a list of the headlines that had appeared in the newspapers serving the Cleveland area. Sheppard had to make the Court take notice of the highly unusual circumstances surrounding his trial. His brief stated, "In quantum of reported material, virulence of content and recklessness of method we believe the publicity in the case at bar to far transcend any other case heretofore decided by this Court."[9]

Then the brief outlined three ways in which the publicity had hampered Sheppard's right to a fair trial. First, pretrial publicity not only forced his arrest but also "precluded the assembly of an impartial jury." The publicity surrounding the case was in such a large quantity that printed stories alone filled five scrapbooks, which were introduced as evidence in the lower courts. These lower courts noted the unusually high media interest in the case. Dr. Sheppard's brief on several occasions used a "circus" or "carnival" metaphor to describe what took place at trial: "Certainly all that is implicit in the bacchanalia of a 'Roman Holiday' is directly out of phase with the serious and ordered decorum which is supposed to be the controlling environment of our American criminal trials."[10]

The second point of which Sheppard tried to convince the Court was that the publicity during the trial had made it impossible to maintain an impartial jury. As a supporting example, Sheppard's brief made special note of a story appearing in the *Cleveland Press* during the trial, a story the state had dismissed as "inane and innocuous" reporting.

> On November 24, 1954, as the prosecution's case drew to a close, the *Press* bannered the asserted fact that Marilyn had viewed Dr. Sam as a "Jekyll-Hyde." The expected testimony of the "bombshell witness" was set forth on page one: Thomas Weigle, Marilyn's cousin, was ready to reveal the following day that she had used this exact term in describing the duality of her husband. Of course in no jurisdiction in the United States (including Ohio) would such testimony have been admissible if it were available; and of course Thomas Weigle did not, when he did take the stand, offer such testimony. Nonetheless, on November 24 the jurors were in their homes in the evening, and many of them received the *Cleveland Press*, an evening newspaper.[11]

Sheppard's third contention was that the publicity generated by the *Cleveland Press* alone (both before and during the trial) had been sufficient to deprive him of due process of law. To this end, the brief recounted a statement made through the *Cleveland Press* by Cleveland Homicide Bureau Chief David Kerr that Sheppard was a "bare-faced liar" and that Kerr would have been able to solve the case in four hours had he been on the scene: "This statement was issued by Kerr in Miami, where he had been vacationing and where he had been able to discern that Dr. Sheppard was the guilty party — by *reading the newspaper!*"[12]

On February 28, 1966, oral argument was held before the United States Supreme Court. Dr. Sheppard's position could be essentially summed up in this exchange between the Court and Bailey:

THE COURT: What effect did the publicity . . . have to so prejudice the community that he could not get a fair trial, a fair jury?

MR. BAILEY: I think the damage was this, Your Honor — and that is why in my brief I have suggested that this does not fall squarely within the cases you have earlier decided in the same general area: There was no confession in this case. There was no criminal record announced. There was no preliminary hearing at which evidence was taken and then broadcast. There was begun, initially by Mr. Selzer and then picked up by other newspapers — the news media — the notion that Dr. Sheppard was "hiding the evidence." It is implicit in all of the publicity, and especially in those editorials that were published during this period, and I believe that it conditioned

108

the community to find him guilty unless he could prove his innocence. For that reason, I think that the publicity was so prejudicial as to have required a continuance or change of venue. At that point, either remedy might have been of tremendous help.

The Court agreed with Bailey's argument and in its opinion focused intensely on the lack of decorum on the part of the news media within the trial courtroom itself. The opinion described the environment in the courtroom: "Their movement in and out of the courtroom often caused so much confusion that, despite the loudspeaker system installed in the courtroom, it was difficult for the witnesses and counsel to be heard. Furthermore, the reporters clustered within the bar of the small courtroom made confidential talk among Sheppard and his counsel almost impossible during the proceedings."[13]

The widespread prejudicial publicity convinced the Court that Sheppard was entitled to a new trial: "Indeed every court that has considered the case, save the court that tried it, has deplored the manner in which the news media inflamed and prejudiced the public."[14] The Court's opinion set out several "suggestions" to lower courts to help counteract prejudicial publicity and avoid the "carnival atmosphere" that took place at Dr. Sheppard's trial. First, the trial judge should adopt strict rules governing the use of the courtroom by the news media and closely regulate in-court conduct. Second, the court should "insulate the witnesses." Third, the court should make an "effort to control the release of leads, information, and gossip to the press by police officers, witnesses, and the counsel for both sides." Fourth, "where there is a reasonable likelihood that prejudicial news prior to trial will prevent a fair trial, the judge should continue the case until the threat abates. . . ." Fifth, alternatively the judge could "transfer it to another county not so permeated with publicity." Sixth, the judge could sequester the jury.[15] Justice Tom Clark clearly put the onus on trial judges to "protect their processes from prejudicial outside interferences."[16]

In the end, the Sheppard case, a landmark ruling, was a diatribe against all forms of prejudicial publicity, not just television — even though, the year before hearing the Sheppard appeal, the Supreme Court had issued its missive specifically on televised cases. The Sheppard case demonstrates that publicity problems are likely in high-profile trials — problems unrelated to the presence of a television camera.

SUPREME INTERVENTION: LIGHTS, CAMERA . . . CUT

The Supreme Court specifically addressed the notion of televised trials on two separate occasions. The first came in 1965, when the obtrusiveness and novelty of early television equipment caused a disturbance in the trial of Texas businessman Billie Sol Estes, who faced swindling charges. Portions of the proceedings were televised, and on appeal of his conviction, Estes argued that the presence of television prejudiced his case. The justices seemed to suggest that the presence of television cameras was inherently prejudicial, and thus defendants would not have to prove specific damage to their cases arising out of the coverage. One insightful notion in the case came in Justice John Harlan's concurring opinion; he predicted that "the day may come when television will have become so commonplace an affair in the daily life of the average person as to dissipate all reasonable likelihood that its use in courtrooms may disparage the judicial process."[17]

Harlan's prediction came to fruition in the Court's second major pronouncement on cameras. In *Chandler v. Florida*,[18] two former police officers on trial in Miami challenged Florida's newly adopted rules that allowed television coverage. They claimed that the mere presence of cameras at their trial rendered the case unfair. The Court rejected the notion that televising the proceedings automatically tainted the trial, even when the defendants objected to the telecast. In fact, the Court said that *Estes* "does not stand as an absolute ban on any experimentation with an evolving technology, which, in terms of modes of

111

mass communication, was in its relative infancy in 1964, and is, even now, in a state of continuing change."[19]

FIRST AMENDMENT IMPLICATIONS

The news media and others are quick to play the First Amendment card in response to unfavorable situations. The media rely specifically on the Amendment's guarantee of a free press.[20] Strictly speaking, neither *Estes* nor *Chandler* even hinted that the news media have a constitutional right to set up cameras in a courtroom. In fact, *Chandler* clearly leaves the decision to the states and their individual courts. The media's right to be present (as opposed to the right to televise the proceedings), however, is guaranteed by the First Amendment and has been since 1980. In that year, the Supreme Court carved out an independent right on the part of the media and the public to attend criminal trials.[21] The Court subsequently made clear that the jury selection process was likewise open to the media and the public,[22] and then extended the right of access to cover preliminary proceedings as well.[23] First Amendment advocates like to view television in the courts as a logical extension of the access cases. After all, if the goal of an open court is to allow the citizenry to witness the proceedings, what better way than through available technology? Yet, this does not suggest that televised proceedings (as well as extensive coverage outside the proceedings) do not present problems with respect to keeping the trial fair for the participants. In fact, this challenge is at the heart of the conflict between the First Amendment and the Sixth Amendment.

A FAIR AND PUBLIC TRIAL

The Sixth Amendment to the United States Constitution provides the accused in a criminal case several guarantees. Principal among them is the right to a "speedy and public trial, by an impartial jury. . . ."[24] These provisions and the others encompassed in the Amendment can be characterized under the rubric of "a fair trial." Much of the criticism surrounding the presence of cameras in the courtroom hovers on the notion that somehow the accused's fair trial rights will be compromised by the television coverage. Critics charge that lawyers, judges, and even witnesses will alter their performances in order to appear better on camera, sometimes causing a detrimental effect on the accused's case. CNN's Bob Furnad disagrees: "I don't buy that [cameras] have affected their performance. The attorneys are playing to the jury." Court TV conducted its own study of 277 judges who had permitted the network to cover a trial in their courtrooms. According to the report, "98 percent of the judges agreed that the presence of

Court TV's cameras had not impeded the fairness of the judicial process."[25] Court TV correspondent Dan Abrams, the reporter assigned to cover the Simpson criminal and civil trials and a regular commentator about the case for NBC's *Today*, also thinks the criticism is unfair. He says the "theatrics" by some of the participants would have gone on even without a camera present. "It was the media attention that this case received outside the courtroom that may have affected some of the attorneys."

The concept of a public trial can be viewed as a check on the third branch of government — the judiciary. As the late Chief Justice Warren Burger noted in *Richmond Newspapers v. Virginia*, it "hopefully promotes confidence in the fair administration of justice."[26] A value can be ascribed to the observation that "the means used to achieve justice must have the support derived from public acceptance of both the process and its results."[27] Burger's opinion also signaled an important note about the role of the media.

Instead of acquiring information about trials by first-hand observation or by word of mouth from those who attended, people now acquire it chiefly through the print and electronic media. In a sense, this validates the media claim of functioning as surrogates for the public. While media representatives enjoy the same right of access as the public, they are often provided special seating and priority of entry so that they may report what people in attendance have seen and heard.[28]

Chief Justice Burger was never viewed as a friend to the media, yet even he recognized the necessity of media access to the proceedings. Accordingly, it is not so much of a stretch to envision a First Amendment that condones televised proceedings as a matter of right — subject, of course, to other compelling needs to the contrary (a notion already woven throughout First Amendment law). As CNN's vice president of public relations, Steve Haworth, observed, "Court is supposed to be open to anybody who can get to it. Viewers can now get to it through a camera. I think it's a natural extension of what the founding fathers meant by mandating that trials be held in open court." Nonetheless, many of the policy arguments defending televised proceedings have become embattled in the aftermath of the Simpson case.

"TRIAL OF THE CENTURY"

"Every day the network struggles and every producer struggles with putting on the air two things: what the audience needs to know and what they want to know. Sometimes it is more need to know; other times there's less need to know and there's time for more want to know. O. J. Simpson is clearly a 'want to know.' It's not

115

a need to know." Those sentiments, expressed by CNN's Bob Furnad, rang true in at least one regard: The American public wanted to know about O. J. Simpson. In some cases, the audience could not get enough. Continuous coverage was available on CNN, Court TV, and the E! Entertainment Channel. Additionally, in Los Angeles local stations' coverage ranged from hourly updates and daily specials to continuous. For CNN, the proof of the public's interest in the case was in the numbers. The news division's spokesman, Steve Haworth, described the audience this way:

> Our O. J. Simpson trial coverage audience has probably averaged about five times the normal daytime audience. It's gone from two or three times to ten times depending on the interest level of the particular witness. So, quantitatively, we are dealing with a much larger daytime audience than normal. This is not a fringe of groupies. This is an average of two-plus million households viewing at a time. That's not a cume of all those who tune in during the day or a week or a month. At any point in time during the trial, we're delivering it to two million viewers — households.

Qualitatively, Haworth found the audience to be "more female than audiences at other times of the day and it tend[ed] to skew somewhat older."

The initial decision to run the O. J. Simpson trial live on both CNN and Court TV was not a difficult one for either organization. Both networks knew it was of enormous interest to the audience. Court TV obviously thrives on courtroom drama that delivers an audience, but for CNN, other programming concerns were present. According to Furnad, "It was just real clear that we were going to commit to doing it, that we were prepared to preempt it for news as warranted. We preempted it for Bosnia and obviously Oklahoma [bombing] — that was a no-brainer. We preempted it for things like the senate vote on the balanced budget amendment — things that really upset the audience by their phone calls, but things we thought the audience needed to know."

For Haworth, the O. J. Simpson trial was an important one in many respects, not just in terms of ratings points. "It's got all the ingredients of late twentieth-century America: Race, spousal abuse or allegations which link to all issues, fallen hero, media hero, and, of course, the personality of the individual that makes it all the more intriguing to people." News executives at CNN knew the trial would be a long one, but they maintain that duration was not a factor. The actual length, however, was a surprise for Bob Furnad. "Our first guess [of the timing of the verdict] was summer (May-June), and then it just kept getting longer and longer."

PRETRIAL PUBLICITY OR CAMERAS IN THE COURTROOM – THE REAL CULPRIT?

Just days after the double murder in Brentwood, it became apparent that the relationship between the media and the courts would deteriorate precipitously during the case. On the June 26, 1994, broadcast of ABC's *This Week with David Brinkley*, the veteran news anchor set the stage of events with his opening:

> The plain facts were melodramatic enough. A famous, admired American figure — O. J. Simpson — accused of two murders, one of them his former wife, riding the streets of Los Angeles, holding a gun to his own head, police cars following to keep a watch on him while millions watched on television. He surrendered.
>
> Some of the press and television then dived overboard stark naked, reporting rumors as news, in some cases simply making up stories, interviewing people who knew nothing or what little they did know was wrong. The *New York Times* asked, "Are we journalists or garbage collectors?" The publicity bath was so enormous that a grand jury exposed to all

of this had to be dismissed, while almost everybody listened in on what had become a grand national intercom.[29]

The media frenzy had clearly begun and would not let up until after the verdict some sixteen months later. Part of the problem identified early on was alluded to by Leo Wolinsky, metro editor of the *Los Angeles Times*, in a pretaped interview for the Brinkley show. He said, "The legitimate media has to be very careful of what they publish because people are out there in the streets. The tabloids are out there — both tabloid television and tabloid newspapers — paying big money for information now."[30] Paying for interviews is considered an unconscionable act by most journalistic organizations. CNN's Steve Haworth calls it "reprehensible" and says it gives legitimate news organizations a bad name: "CNN does not pay anyone for an interview because the paying taints it, and I think that's a crucial variant."

Under the First Amendment, the press is free from government control and is not subject to any type of licensing. That is a tremendous right and one that far outweighs any of the negative consequences. Nonetheless, the downside is that almost any organizations can claim to be part of the press — or media — and thus avail itself of the protections enveloped in the First Amendment. In addition to that quagmire is another, more complicated, image problem.

119

Many Americans simply lump all such organizations together when they are thinking about this amorphous entity called "the media." As a result, the sins of unsavory journalists are blamed on the conscientious reporters as well. Some critics, such as the *Los Angeles Times*'s Howard Rosenberg, see it differently, finding that all coverage especially on television — "is really an extension of something that's been happening in this country for at least five years and that is this terrible fungus called 'tabloid.' And it's just spreading all over the place . . . and most of the coverage of the O. J. Simpson-Goldman story has been an example of that."[31] The "fungus" that Rosenberg speaks of is the basis for a great debate over what has been called "infotainment" — the blurring of the lines of distinction between news and entertainment programs (this phenomenon is discussed more fully in chapter seven).

Networks providing gavel-to-gavel coverage are quick to point out that what most people regard as distasteful regarding trial coverage has nothing to do with the camera in the courtroom, rather it is an indictment of what is going on outside the courthouse. CNN's Haworth says "that very quiet, almost unnoticeable camera up in the corner of the ceiling is much less impactful in those kinds of arenas than the gaggle of press from *Hard Copy* to *Inside Edition* to the more legitimate media that gathered outside on the steps." Anyone watching what transpired outside the O. J. Simpson courtroom would reach the same conclusion, according to CNN's Furnad: "You go to L.A. and see a whole parking lot across from the courthouse taken up by television equipment. How else could you describe that but a circus? The fact is that unlike the days when there was no electronic media, it was only the pencil press, we are not invisible anymore. We are not low-key and barely there. When we go there with trucks, satellite dishes, and with the number of people it takes to get this stuff on and off the air, it creates a circus." Court TV's Dan Abrams adds that the famous O. J. Simpson chase, which was televised live nationally, "was such a national media event that it would be foolhardy to not have at least anticipated the possibility that this was going to be a huge media event."

The debate over cameras in the courtroom is often seen as self-serving for the media, but Court TV's position paper makes an important point about such coverage: "It allows the participants in a democracy to judge for themselves how well the government institution that makes the most fundamental decision that any government makes — liberty or prison — is working."[32] As Steve Haworth sees it, without cameras in court the best viewers can hope for (straight from the source) are the "snippets that one party or the other thinks are going to work to their advantage."

INSIDE JUDGE ITO'S COURTROOM

California is one of those states with permanent rules allowing cameras into civil and criminal courts on both trial and appellate levels. Nonetheless, judges have wide discretion in the scope of the coverage. Early on in the O. J. Simpson case, it was clear that Judge Lance Ito was wavering about permitting the pool camera to remain in the courtroom. Several incidents involving the media, including an inadvertent glimpse of a juror in the jury box, forbidden territory for the camera, prompted a threat by the judge to pull the plug on coverage, and the threat was taken seriously by media organizations. Bob Furnad said CNN was concerned because losing the ability to carry the proceedings live would have been a great disappointment for the audience. "There was a great expectation on the part of viewers. There was a great expectation on our part in terms of a continuing news story that was going to go on for some months, and we were very, very concerned." Court TV's Dan Abrams had a courtroom vantage point, and he, too, "thought [Ito] was quite serious about the possibility of not allowing it."

Court TV also reported that Judge Ito himself recognized the benefit of the live coverage when he noted that any "damage done by the erroneous local news report about some forensic test results had been mitigated by his own comments about it in open court — because those comments had been televised. 'It is to the [defendant's] benefit that the false reports in the press have been unmasked' on television, [Ito] stated."[33] After the trial, Judge Ito granted a rare interview to a university student whom he told that he favored televised coverage and believed that cameras belonged in the courtroom.

THE AFTERMATH

Legal scholars, commentators, and other pundits will continue to kick around the benefits and drawbacks of post-O. J. television coverage. Even before the trial ended, some debris began to fall. The judge in South Carolina who was assigned to the Susan Smith trial banned television cameras from his courtroom. Smith was charged in the drowning deaths of her two young sons. She had further drawn attention to herself by pleading nationwide for their safe return, claiming that the children had been taken by a black man who had carjacked her vehicle while the boys were still inside. Despite the lack of live television, the media were at the trial en masse. According to CNN's Bob Furnad, "What you have in the Susan Smith trial is that they closed a whole city block just so that these platforms built across from the courthouse for reporters to be seen with the courthouse behind them can be there."

Even in Los Angeles, trial judge Stanley Weisberg not only banned live television from the retrial of Lyle and Eric Menendez but also made the public street near the courthouse off-limits to reporters with cameras or recording equipment.

If anything, the Simpson trial left us with one clear revelation: Americans are intrigued by the legal process. The quantifiable measurement of television ratings is an indication, but even reporters who cover trials, like Dan Abrams, were surprised at the level of commitment the viewers gave to the case. "Once the preliminary hearing began, it became clear that this was a major news story, but what surprised me was the ability that this trial had to sustain interest over a period of nine months. . . . During the DNA testimony, it was still the lead story in the local news in Los Angeles."

Blocking televised coverage does nothing to further the fair trial rights of criminal defendants. As the Susan Smith case and countless other high-profile cases have shown, the media will always have a presence. Keeping the lens cap on the camera will only fuel the innuendo and inflammatory reporting that history has demonstrated will inevitably occur. Therein lies the benefit of the live camera in the courtroom. As CNN's Steve Haworth observed:

In other words, it helps cut through the inflamed rhetoric of those who use partial bits and pieces of information for their own purposes — be they sensational media outlets who will take snippets of trials that may or may not reflect what actually transpired or be they people who have a cross to bear one way or the other vis-à-vis the outcome. I think it's an important and definitely a positive complement to open courts in general, and it's a natural extension of democracy in a media age.

C-SPAN's Bruce Collins labels the aftermath of the O. J. Simpson case an overreaction. The case was "truly an anomaly," says Collins. "There was nothing like it before. So we have an anomaly that is affecting decisions on some of the most ordinary cases that should be presented to the public with absolutely no problem." Collins points out that the Simpson case did not signal a trend and that part of the problem with the trial was that it took place in "the heart of the entertainment capital of the world."

O. J. EPILOGUE

Judge Hiroshi Fujisaki, the trial judge in the civil case against O. J. Simpson, foreclosed media problems in that case by banning all television cameras from the courtroom. Additionally, he barred all lawyers, witnesses, and other parties involved in the trial from speaking publicly about the case. By his August 23, 1996, order, Fujisaki demonstrated that the televised Simpson criminal trial would have a lasting effect on the future of television in the courtroom. His ruling stated:

> The Court has concluded from the experience of the criminal trial of this defendant concerning the same essential factual circumstances, that the electronic coverage of the trial significantly diverted and distracted the participants therein, it appearing that the conduct of witnesses and counsel were unduly influenced by the presence of the electronic media. This conduct was manifested in various ways such as playing to the camera, gestures, outbursts by counsel and witnesses, in the courtroom and thereafter outside of the courthouse, presenting a circus atmosphere to the trial.[34]

The judge's ruling further chastised the media for taking comments out of context in the criminal trial and broadcasting them in "every format imaginable, particularly newscasts at all hours." In keeping in place a "gag order" on the participants in the civil case, the judge balanced First Amendment considerations against what he called "the duty of this court to conduct the trial in a neutral and detached environment necessary to insulate rational argument and dispassionate decision making from the passions that will inevitably arise from extra-judicial commentary on the part of those who are hereby constrained." The Sheppard case, referenced earlier in this chapter, levied this obligation on trial judges.

Many members of the legal profession and the general public have misgivings about allowing televised coverage of trials. No doubt the O. J. Simpson criminal trial only fuels the criticism. Sadly, many (perhaps even most) Americans support Judge Fujisaki's order because the media debacle of the criminal trial is too fresh in their minds. Yet, the taxpayers of California are paying for that court system in Santa Monica, and most cannot see their tax dollars in action. Imagine the outrage if the local city council in Santa Monica suddenly declared that it had tired of the spread of misinformation and thus its meetings would be no longer open to cameras and city council members would no longer speak to the media about any of the issues raised. The public would not stand for it. For some reason, though, when the court — also a branch of government — behaves that way, the public not only tolerates such action, it actually applauds it.

5

Safeguarding Unpopular Expression

"At the heart of the First Amendment lies the principle that each person should decide for him or herself the ideas and beliefs deserving of expression, consideration, and adherence."

— *Turner Broadcasting System v. F.C.C.*, 1994

The founders of this nation were renegades and rogues. Their views were not the ones most cherished in their native England. Consequently, when they set up the governing structure of this nation, they wanted to ensure that people like themselves would not face similar oppression here. What they constructed was a remarkable doctrine embodied in a rich document that could grow with the ages and yet retain its basic form. The Bill of Rights was a way to keep government from becoming all-powerful, and the First Amendment was crucial to this vision.

Throughout its history the First Amendment

has been used to keep those whose views clashed with the majority's free from persecution — with varying degrees of success. Sometimes it has worked — but sometimes at great cost. Nonetheless, it is a point that is often lost on the majority. Proponents of the notion that unpopular viewpoints must be heard often have to send a reminder notice. Justice William J. Brennan Jr. eloquently sent one in *Texas v. Johnson* when he wrote: "If there is a bedrock principle underlying the First Amendment, it is that the government may not prohibit the expression of an idea simply because society finds the idea itself offensive or disagreeable."[1]

The case, which is discussed fully later in this chapter, served as a good venue for this reminder because clearly the issue involved — the right to desecrate the American flag as a form of protest — is an unpopular view. Many people have an understandably difficult time differentiating the conduct from the symbolism — and even more difficulty discerning how we all gain in terms of our liberty by protecting such activities. Stated differently, how would we lose if protection for these undesirable acts disappeared?

Little danger exists that First Amendment rights will dissipate overnight. No one is going to suggest that the nation suspend the premier amendment in the Bill of Rights. What does happen, though, and what is happening, is a gradual erosion of rights over time. The change is so gradual that most people do not even notice until they are looking for the protection that once was available and find it is no longer there. Consider, for example, the First Amendment rights of public school students. In 1969 the U.S. Supreme Court boosted the constitutional rights of minors enrolled in public schools in a way that beautifully illustrated the power of the individual, even one yet to reach the age of majority, in the face of government control.

The case involved a brother and sister from Des Moines, Iowa, who decided to show their disdain toward American policy in Vietnam by wearing black armbands to school. After noticing this apparel, the school administrator ordered them not to wear it again on the premises. The next day the pair defied the order and once again wore the armbands. The principal immediately suspended the two students for disobeying his rule. With the help of their father, the siblings brought suit against the school district, claiming their suspension violated their rights of free expression. The case went up the appellate ladder and ultimately landed at the Supreme Court. The Court recognized the students' conduct as expressive. They were wearing the armbands to make a statement — a political one — and if any speech deserves great protection, political speech does. The majority opinion contained an often-quoted line about how public school students do not "shed their constitutional rights to freedom of speech or expression at the schoolhouse gate."[2]

For a while that pithy maxim seemed like a rule, but as the makeup of the Court began to change in the 1980s, so did that notion. In 1986 a high school junior in Bethel, Washington, learned the hard way that the schoolhouse gate was no longer the line in the sand. Matthew Fraser thought it would be funny to use some cleverly placed sexual metaphors in a nomination speech for a friend running for student government. The school's principal did not find it as amusing as the student population did. The U.S. Supreme Court upheld Fraser's suspension. Chief Justice Warren Burger wrote, "The undoubted freedom to advocate unpopular and controversial views in school must be balanced against the society's countervailing interest in teaching students the boundaries of socially appropriate behavior."[3] Burger said that teachers and students in the audience were offended by Fraser's remarks. Justice John Paul Stevens dissented and questioned if the Court was in the best position to determine if the remarks were offensive, particularly in light of the fact that the student on whose behalf the remarks were made was elected by the student body.[4]

Two years later a high school newspaper editor sued after two pages of her last edition of the school year were excised by the principal. After receiving page proofs from the paper's adviser, the principal found that two stories presented problems. The first troublesome story was about three students in the high school who were pregnant. The story did not mention the girls' names, but the principal believed that some students might figure out who they were anyway. The second story at issue was an interview with a named female student who made some rather harsh accusations against her father. Because the father had not been interviewed for the story, the principal decided to kill the piece. The Court ruled that the school was perfectly within its rights to stifle the stories.[5] The justices further noted that a newspaper is not a public forum for purposes of the First Amendment.

Read in toto, these cases show a deterioration of the rights enjoyed by public school students. That is precisely how the government can continue to chip away at First Amendment rights, little by little — and the victims are not always under the age of eighteen.

Chiseling away rights is sometimes made easier for the courts or the legislatures when the public has had its fill of the message that someone wants to have suppressed. People are less concerned about First Amendment rights when they are fed up with material they feel should not be protected anyway, such as programming by the numerous "shock jocks" and talk show hosts now inhabiting radio and television.

TALK RADIO

In the 1970s AM radio dominated the airwaves and FM radio lingered as mostly a place to put experimental and educational stations. Then things changed dramatically. FM stereo made it clear that music was best heard over that band, and gradually AM stations lost their appeal. Articles appeared for several years in the trade press forecasting AM radio's demise. Then things changed again. This time the music was replaced by talk — not just any talk, but talk that made people want to listen. In fact, it is not a stretch to suggest that talk radio single-handedly rescued the AM band. By the 1980s, pop psychologists, sex therapists, and a new breed of current affairs hosts surfaced and, with the help of syndication, found their way across America's airwaves.

Instant celebrity came to many broadcasters who had for years toiled in obscurity, with Rush Limbaugh leading the pack. What's more, many people who had never been behind a microphone professionally, such as G. Gordon Liddy and Oliver North, now found themselves immersed in a national daily forum allowing them to express their opinions on myriad subjects. As more and more of these new talk show hosts hit the airwaves, the key to success became vitriol aimed mostly at those in public life not espousing a similar ideology.

Caustic hosts have become such a mainstay of today's talk radio format that some people are concerned that their acid-tongued messages may pose a threat to democratic principles. What is more, a flurry of misinformation sails across America's airwaves now on a daily basis. Rumor and innuendo have become easy substitutes for facts on some of these programs. Howard Kurtz, a reporter for the *Washington Post* and author of *Hot Air: All Talk All the Time*, found that not all the banter is innocuous. "The extremist hosts can certainly play a damaging role by spreading unsubstantiated garbage and whipping people up, playing us against them, and exploiting divisions in society," said Kurtz. However, he stops short of blaming the hate talkers for inciting groups to take illegal action.

In 1994, after G. Gordon Liddy advised his listeners that if they intended to shoot FBI or ATF agents they should aim for the head because otherwise the bullet might be deflected by protective vests, a controversial storm erupted that caused some people to question the lack of regulation on such speech. Traditional First Amendment law provides a remedy for inciteful speech, but to ensure the highest degree of protection to speech, a distinction must be made between highly charged rhetoric and speech actually intended to produce illegal action. In 1969 the U.S. Supreme Court decided a case involving a Ku Klux Klan member in

Ohio who had been charged with advocating racial bigotry. The Court's decision, in *Brandenburg v. Ohio*,[6] clarified the fifty-year-old "clear and present danger test"[7] by prohibiting the government from punishing someone who advocates the use of force or other illegal action "except where such advocacy is directed to inciting or producing imminent lawless action and is likely to incite or produce such action."[8] The notion of "clear and present danger" was first articulated in 1919, when Justice Oliver Wendell Holmes wrote that speech could be prohibited only if the words, as used in a particular context, would immediately bring about illegal activity.

Americans should be wary of any restrictions on radio hosts or such hostile speech in other fora, for any such measures would necessarily require a determination made with respect to the content of the speech. As with other content-based regulation, the question then becomes who determines which content is objectionable. Surveys have shown that some people might acquiesce to such restrictions, but Kurtz, who has delved deeply into the talk show issue, finds the notion of regulation to be "a spectacularly bad idea because next week the definition of objectionable speech may change. This would lead us down a slippery slope and be damaging to the First Amendment."

Talk radio restrictions would also curtail the enormous power of the medium to contribute to healthy debate in society. Once almost entirely local in origin, talk programs are gaining in popularity. And syndicators and networks, recognizing the vast audience potential, have extended the reach of many shows from coast to coast. Diane Rehm has hosted a talk radio program on Washington's National Public Radio affiliate WAMU since 1979. Now, her show can be heard nationwide on NPR affiliates. A veteran host, Rehm recognizes that the genre has changed. "When I first got started twenty years ago, I really had great hope that talk radio was going to assist in people's understanding of each other. That it was somehow going to take the place of the back fence. It sounds quaint right now, considering what it's become." Rehm observed that "the level of anger and hostility has gone up" on talk radio and "along the way has gotten in the way of people's ability to think clearly and rationally about the very complicated issues that we're dealing with."

Talk radio at its best can provide the opportunity for a discussion of public issues. In a sense, it is a modern manifestation of the marketplace of ideas concept first popularized by John Milton in the 1600s, further developed two centuries later by John Stuart Mill, and eventually infused as a concept in First Amendment law by Justice Oliver Wendell Holmes. As Howard Kurtz has pointed out, "Talk radio has the unique power to mobilize people against hot-button issues — a congressional pay raise, national health-care policy, or affirmative action." Hosts need to be acutely aware of this power and control for it. Diane Rehm found an example of this on her own show when President Clinton announced that he would stand by Zoe Baird, his nominee for attorney general, despite her problems with not paying taxes for a domestic employee. On the day of that announcement, "when I simply opened the phones . . . the calls flooded, saying this is outrageous. She has to be gone, and two days later she was gone. What happened on my program was happening on other stations." Moreover, Rehm said, she did not generate this sentiment. She merely asked her listeners what they thought should happen.

At its worst, talk radio can "create a climate where all types of intolerance can thrive," according to media critic Kurtz. Rehm, too, is concerned about how rational debate has in many corners of the spectrum given way to extreme right-wing or left-wing rhetoric. She believes it is "affecting how we see each other, talk to each other, engage with each other and certainly affecting our political discourse." Rehm recognized that many talk show hosts "have a political agenda and are pushing toward that means."

Rehm views it as the host's responsibility to ensure against the proliferation of misinformation on the radio. To illustrate the point, she recalled a listener who called in to her program shortly after the suicide of White House aide

Vincent Foster. The caller claimed to have the real story behind the death of the White House counsel. Rehm asked the caller if what he knew was fact or rumor. When the caller informed her that he had no facts, she told him that he would not be on the air. Rehm says she caught flack for not letting the caller air his thoughts, but she would not change her position. "If I as a host not only permit but encourage that kind of rumor gathering and distribution, then I'm part of the problem." But she also understood that her position is "odd" in terms of talk radio today.

Rehm places the blame for the behavior of some hosts squarely on management. Talk radio is big business, and the push for the greatest distribution of programming is what drives the business. Consequently, if controversial behavior brings in money, the more outrageous the better. As an example, she cited the incident involving veteran New York talk show host Bob Grant, who was fired from ABC Radio after he made a distasteful remark about the late commerce secretary Ron Brown, who at the time was missing and presumed dead in a plane crash. Grant said, "My hunch is he is the one survivor. I just have that hunch maybe because, at heart, I'm a pessimist." Shortly thereafter, Grant was picked up by another New York station, WOR, and was given the green light to "keep going."

BALANCING THE AIRWAVES

Howard Kurtz says he is not bothered by the fact that approximately 70 percent of talk radio hosts are on the conservative side of the political spectrum (in fact, he sees that figure as "dictated by the free market"). Obviously, neither are the conservative hosts. G. Gordon Liddy has said the hosts from the right "are attempting to provide some balance to the overwhelmingly liberal bias of the institutional media."[9] Liddy views the number of radio outlets offering such a wide variety of programs as proof of the balance of viewpoints.

Indeed, the tables may once again turn in terms of the dominant ideological bent of talk radio hosts. Kurtz has predicted that "people may grow tired of extreme ranters and ravers" but that talk on the radio will most likely continue to grow. Rehm agreed: "We may be reaching . . . a level of awareness about what's happening out there and a calling into question the extent that in the name of free speech this whole idea of unfiltered information" is permitted on the air. Rehm is "beginning to wonder whether we've seen the crest of the G. Gordon Liddys . . . the Limbaughs, the Imuses, and the Howard Sterns." Both Don Imus and Howard Stern have enjoyed the fruits of national attention through their antics both on and off the air.

Imus made national headlines when he spoke at the Radio and Television Correspondents Dinner on March 21, 1996. His speech contained numerous barbs aimed at journalists and politicos, but he caught the most flack for his unrelenting cuts on President Clinton and the First Lady. White House Press Secretary Mike McCurry even asked C-SPAN, the only outlet to carry the remarks live and in full, to not rebroadcast it. C-SPAN did not oblige. Howard Stern, whose show is produced by Infinity Broadcasting, has crossed the line of decency numerous times, resulting in the accrual of FCC fines in the seven figures. The FCC has been given authority by Congress and the courts to regulate indecent speech in broadcasting by channeling it to particular time periods.

If the tide does turn, it will do so because the market forces it to do so. That is precisely what the First Amendment is designed to protect. The old adage has been resurrected in several forms already in this book and bears repeating: The answer to bad speech is more speech. The marketplace of ideas notion requires that society permit the ideas, no matter how outrageous, hateful, hurtful, or ridiculous they may seem, to enter into the public discourse. The people will sort out for themselves what is useful and what is not. To require anything else would necessitate a filter for content and thus the problems associated with censorship. Eventually, if the market for raunch dries up, raunch will disappear.

THE OUTLOOK IS FAIR

Some of those concerned about the proliferation of unchecked extremist viewpoints on the air argue in favor of government regulation to achieve balance. They harken back to a time prior to the mid-1980s when such regulation was embodied in the Fairness Doctrine. The governmental interest of fairness in broadcasting dates almost as far back as the industry itself. The earliest regulations governing broadcasting mandated that licensees operate in the "public interest, convenience, and necessity."[10]

The Fairness Doctrine officially came about in 1959 when Congress amended Section 315 of the Communications Act of 1934, although the idea of prescribing some fairness rules had been kicked around during the previous decade.[11] The Fairness Doctrine as envisioned by the FCC essentially required two things. First, broadcasters must affirmatively seek out controversial issues of public importance to their coverage area. Second, when covering controversial public issues, broadcasters must seek a balance of opposing viewpoints. The commission gave great latitude to the broadcasters to decide which issues warranted such coverage.

The doctrine was controversial from its inception. Broadcasters viewed it as governmental control over content and thus anathema to the

First Amendment. Proponents saw it as a way to ensure that the airwaves, a public resource, would inure to the benefit of the public. Broadcasters unsuccessfully challenged it on those grounds in the late 1960s. The Supreme Court saw it differently. In the majority opinion in a consolidated case involving the Red Lion Broadcasting Co. and the Radio Television News Directors Association (RTNDA) as parties, Justice Byron White observed:

> Believing that the specific application of the Fairness Doctrine in *Red Lion*, and the promulgation of the regulations in *RTNDA*, are both authorized by Congress and enhance rather than abridge the freedoms of speech and press protected by the First Amendment, we hold them valid and constitutional. . . . [12]

The Court went on to find that the creation of the Fairness Doctrine was a "legitimate exercise of congressionally delegated authority."[13] This latter observation eventually became troublesome. In the mid-1980s the commission sought to abandon enforcement of the doctrine as deregulation fever swept through Washington. In two separate court decisions from the United States Court of Appeals for the District of Columbia Circuit, that court found that the Fairness Doctrine might not have ever been legislatively intended by Congress.[14] In fact, the measure was simply a creation of the Federal

142

Communications Commission. In essence, what the FCC made, the FCC could destroy, and this is precisely what happened. On August 4, 1987, the commission abolished the Fairness Doctrine. Congressional efforts to resurrect it proved fruitless. One such attempt, a few weeks before the Christmas recess in 1987, prompted a standoff between congressional proponents of the measure and President Ronald Reagan. House Commerce Committee Chair John Dingell (D-Michigan) attached the codification of the Fairness Doctrine to an omnibus appropriations bill, but backed off when President Reagan threatened an eleventh-hour veto that would have kept Congress in session over the Christmas holiday.[15]

Although some members of Congress and some others would like to see the Fairness Doctrine return, most commentators agree that it would be a bad idea. Despite the 1969 Supreme Court decision upholding the constitutionality of the Fairness Doctrine, any such rules mandating programming put government hands where they should not be — wrapped around editorial decisions over content. NPR's Diane Rehm found no indication that a Fairness Doctrine would rise again. Instead, she said, talk show hosts must "take it on [themselves] to ensure that what goes out is reasonable and, to a certain extent, balanced."

As for overall balance, the marketplace can correct itself, and according to Rehm, "the marketplace is already beginning to resound." For example, she pointed to the removal of Mike Siegel of KING in Seattle, Washington. Rehm said Siegel "led the campaign against [former House Speaker] Tom Foley with some absolutely false rumors and then again on this mayor of Seattle, he got caught putting the rumor out on the air." Rehm said she has enormous faith in the American public and believes that the people can take care of the situation themselves, without government control of talk radio.

Whether such radio talk phenomena as Rush Limbaugh will continue to thrive remains to be seen. One element is certain. Limbaugh has learned to use the medium with great skill. As E. J. Dionne, a political columnist for the *Washington Post*, observed in an article that quoted him in the *National Review*, "His message is traditional, but his means are modern." Using rock and roll to segue to and from commercials, Limbaugh has appealed to a younger audience. The audience appetite for the unusual, loud, or bizarre, if not nourished on radio, may be satisfied by turning on the tube.

TAKE OUT THE TRASH

Daytime television channel surfers can attest to the proliferation of talk shows debuting with great regularity on stations all across the country. In fact, the individual credited with creating the format nearly three decades earlier, Phil Donahue, called it quits in 1996 after his ratings declined, due in part to the groundswell of competition. These newer shows have been labeled "tabloid," named for their supermarket print counterparts where innuendo, rumor, sex, and lies are a mainstay of the "news hole." Guests' willingness to air their "dirty laundry" on these programs feeds the tastes of electronic voyeurism that seems to be prevalent in daytime television markets throughout the United States.

Naturally, where controversial programming is found, so too are people who want to clean it up. Advocates of giving daytime television an "enema" have found help from those both inside and outside government and from both sides of the ideological aisle. Senator Joseph I. Lieberman (D-Connecticut) teamed up in 1995 with former education secretary William Bennett to launch a campaign to pressure daytime programmers to clean up the airwaves. The topic is certainly a lively one, as Lieberman's aide Dan Gerstein explained: "The message we kept getting from parents is that they were overwhelmed by the media, and they were being robbed of their ability to control the messages that reached their children."

Lieberman recognized from the feedback that he had touched a political hot button and decided to push it. Legislative assistant Gerstein, the aide handling the issue, said Lieberman launched the campaign against tabloid television and daytime talk shows specifically because "he felt it was the worst of the worst, that it was the edge of the envelope that was being pushed, that it was plunging standards downward." But Lieberman does not see a problem with using his office to pressure television programmers. He saw no potential chilling effect. As Gerstein put it, "Everything with the First Amendment and all constitutional issues is about balance. Where you draw that line between influence [by government] and chilling effect is certainly open to debate, and it's certainly something that's a serious issue worth considering. However, to suggest that a United States senator can't speak his mind — express his opinion — for fear of chilling [the media] boggles the mind. . . ."

Gerstein did not agree that Lieberman was forcing talk show programmers to adjust their shows to meet his objections. "This is not government telling anybody anything," he said. "This is an elected official who happens to be very concerned about this trying to speak out for his constituents and also speaking out as a citizen and as a father." According to Gerstein, Lieberman and Bill Bennett "all along . . . have been saying this is not about censorship, this is about citizenship."

The problem with this line of reasoning in terms of the First Amendment is that casting the debate in terms of citizenship rather than censorship works for every issue involving free expression — flag burning, nude dancing, indecency on the Internet. Many people have difficulty seeing the value of protecting the expression rights of pornographers or journalists who burn their sources, but the value of doing so is sometimes not found in protecting the individuals in the case at hand (although arguably that too has value) but rather in the larger scope of ratifying the protections we as a nation have held sacred for so long. The way Senator Lieberman's office wants to frame this issue is a classic illustration of the central thesis of this book — the gradual erosion of rights mentioned in the opening pages. By moving the discussion away from the free speech implications and toward a laudable goal — in this case, shielding children from smut on television — attention is diverted from the more global issue of censorship in its most basic form — government trying to stop a particular type of expression.

Paul McMasters, a former editor at *USA Today*, is now the First Amendment ombudsman for the Freedom Forum, "a nonpartisan international foundation dedicated to free press, free speech, and free spirit for all people." McMasters is greatly troubled by government officials who use their office to pressure talk programmers. "I could buy that, I guess, if it were just Bill Bennett, but you've got Sam Nunn and Joseph Lieberman standing with ten-foot clubs behind their backs," he said. More is at stake than simply taste, according to McMasters. "It is the height of arrogance, and one of the most undemocratic things that we can do in this country is to start looking down our noses at what people choose to read, to watch, and to listen to." He also recognized the implied threat of government interference, some of which has historically come to fruition. "If anybody doubts that that is a prospect or potential, take a look at the whole debate over the V-chip and violence on television. Senator Paul Simon (D-Illinois) two years [before passage of the Telecommunications Act] started convening hearings telling everybody who would listen and making long apologetic speeches saying, listen we are not having these hearings to talk about legislation. We would never interfere with the First Amendment rights of broadcasters. We just want to raise the issue and raise the profile of the issue so that people will understand how concerned people are." As McMasters is quick to point out, we now have a law requiring V-chip technology in television sets. The V-chip will undoubtedly be used to block out daytime talk as well as prime-time violence (the V-chip will be discussed more fully in chapter eight).

Violence on television and trash talk TV are unpopular in one sense. They form the basis of a great deal of criticism of the medium, and they are usually trotted out as proof of what is wrong with television. Yet, market forces ultimately decide what programming remains on television. And the fact is that enough people watch this type of programming to sustain it, at least for a while. If government seeks to step in and suppress this material before the market can right itself because some have found it offensive, it will run afoul of the First Amendment. As the Freedom Forum's McMasters observed, "to try to dismiss millions of Americans as worthless as far as their rights are concerned simply because they are watching something that is too pedestrian or too vulgar" threatens individual liberty.

Using offensiveness as the grounds for suppressing speech has gotten the government into trouble on past occasions as well, even when the message was relayed symbolically.

A SYMBOL OF THE TIMES

Part of the greatness of this nation is the variety of viewpoints represented from coast to coast. The United States is anything but united on controversial issues, and this is precisely why we need a strong First Amendment — to allow all of us to participate in the debate and to remind us of our common tradition. This first freedom assures us of a ticket to the fight. What happens when we get there is anybody's guess, but each of us is entitled to be a player. One of the most bitter debates fragmenting the country in this decade was over the Supreme Court's sanctioning of the burning of the nation's premier symbol — the American flag.

Schoolchildren salute it and sing songs about it, holidays are fashioned to honor it, and tributes to the fallen are conducted by displaying it midway down the flagpole. The flag stands for America. And for exactly that reason some people have denigrated that symbol as an illustration of their distaste for particular policies or politics in America. Not surprisingly, flag burning raises the ire of a majority of Americans, and laws prohibiting the flag's desecration have been popular. Accordingly, when the Supreme Court said such laws are unconstitutional, many in the nation were filled with rage, and calls to amend the Constitution were answered by Congress. Even some people who revered the First Amendment had trouble allowing this act in protest. Perhaps it takes them back to a dark period in our recent history. Two events — the fight for civil rights and the war in Vietnam — brought the flag-burning issue to the forefront of American constitutional law.

DISRESPECT IN ACTION

Enraged over the shooting death of civil rights activist James Meredith, a young black man in Brooklyn, New York, carried his American flag into a busy intersection and set it on fire. He had just learned about Meredith's killing on a television news broadcast and felt betrayed by a nation at war with itself. When a police officer arrived, the young man admitted igniting the flag in protest of the lack of protection given to Meredith. The officer arrested him under New York's antidesecration law, but he was convicted for his speech rather than for the symbolic expression. Consequently, when the Supreme Court heard the case, the question of the constitutionality of antidesecration statutes could be avoided altogether.

Sidestepping a legal issue usually can be done only for a short time, but the Supreme Court was able to do so two more times before it had to face the issue directly. On one such occasion, the issue was whether a college student violated the law when he hung a flag upside down outside his apartment window with a peace symbol on it constructed out of electrical tape.[16] According to a state court that had earlier heard the case, the Washington law had the purpose of "preserving the national flag as an unalloyed symbol of our country."[17] Because the privately owned flag involved in this case was not permanently destroyed, the Supreme Court declined to reach the larger issue of whether the state's interest was consistent with the First Amendment.

The vagueness of a Massachusetts statute punishing anyone who "treats contemptuously the flag of the United States" saved a resident there quite literally by the seat of his pants, where he had sewn a small flag. Again, sidestepping the real issue of First Amendment protection, the Supreme Court wrote:

Yet in a time of widely varying attitudes and tastes for displaying something as ubiquitous as the United States flag or representations of it, it could hardly be the purpose of the Massachusetts Legislature to make criminal every informal use of the flag. The statutory language under which [the defendant] was charged, however, fails to draw reasonably clear lines between the kinds of non-ceremonial treatment that are criminal and those that are not.[18]

The Court's avoidance of the controversy ended in 1989. That was the year the Court heard the case of a Texas man, Gregory Johnson, who "doused [the American flag] with kerosene and set it on fire" outside the Dallas City Hall in 1984 while the Republican National Convention was under way.[19] After being convicted under a Texas law prohibiting the desecration of a venerated object, Johnson's case was eventually overturned by the Texas Court of Criminal Appeals. That court ruled that Johnson's actions in protest were protected by the First Amendment despite the fact that several witnesses testified that they were "seriously offended" by the burning flag.

When the case reached the United States Supreme Court, the issue was plain: Did Johnson's actions constitute "expressive conduct, permitting him to invoke the First Amendment in challenging his conviction"?[20] Justice William J.

Brennan Jr. wrote the Court's opinion and in it borrowed a notion from an earlier case that the great value of the First Amendment is seen in the protection of dissenting voices. "It may indeed serve its high purpose when it induces a condition of unrest, creates dissatisfaction with conditions as they are, or even stirs people to anger," wrote Brennan, quoting *Terminiello v. Chicago*.[21] The circumstances surrounding Johnson's action were not lost on the Court. Brennan, recognizing that Johnson was protesting the nomination of President Ronald Reagan, wrote: "The expressive, overtly political nature of this conduct was both intentional and overwhelmingly apparent."[22] Yet, the mere act of burning the nation's symbol angered other members of the Court who steadfastly refused to cloak such action in constitutional protection.

In dissent, Chief Justice William H. Rehnquist said, "For more than two hundred years, the American flag has occupied a unique position as the symbol of our nation, a uniqueness that justifies a governmental prohibition against flag burning in a way respondent Johnson did here."[23] Perhaps it was Rehnquist and the other dissenters' feelings that gave encouragement, or it might just have been the political outcry over the decision that prompted some members of Congress to hastily draft a bill outlawing flag desecration.

The Flag Protection Act of 1989 was barely law when Shawn Eichman set a flag ablaze in

Seattle. Others replicated the action in Washington, D.C., and before long the issue was back on the docket of the Supreme Court. The government hoped to show that the new federal law handled the problems the Court had with the Texas statute. According to the government's lawyers, the new act was not intended to suppress the content of messages, rather its purpose was to "protect the physical integrity of the flag under all circumstances. . . ."[24] The Court, in the same configuration as in *Texas v. Johnson*, rejected the government's argument and found that the act was clearly related to suppressing expression and thus a clear violation of the First Amendment.

Immediate calls to amend the Constitution found proponents in Congress, but a Democratic majority kept the measure out. An epilogue to this bit of unpopular speech came in June 1995, when the Republican majority in the Congress attempted to pass a constitutional amendment that would permit criminalizing flag desecration. The amendment passed the House 312 to 120 but was defeated in the Senate in December. The House bill would have allowed the states as well as Congress to criminalize the activity. The Senate version would have permitted only federal criminalization. A similar pattern emerged in June 1997, when the House passed an amendment allowing Congress to outlaw flag burning. Again the Senate votes for passage were not there.

KILLING THE MESSENGER

A troubling notion for publishers and others who transmit information but have no real control over how that information is used is the willingness on the part of individuals and courts to assess liability for the result. The recent lawsuit against the publisher of *Hit Man: A Technical Manual for Independent Contractors* provides an illustration and a First Amendment area that is ripe for erosion. Paladin Enterprises, Inc., published the book in 1983 and sold some 13,000 copies. The publisher's catalog contains the following promotional blurb for the book:

> Rex Feral kills for hire. Some consider him a criminal. Others think him a hero. In truth, he is a lethal weapon aimed at those he hunts. He is a last recourse in these times when laws are so twisted that justice goes unserved. He is a man who feels no twinge of guilt at doing his job. He is a professional killer.
>
> Learn how a pro gets assignments, creates a false identity, makes a disposable silencer, leaves the scene without a trace, watches his mark unobserved, and more. Feral reveals how to get in, do the job, and get out without getting caught. For academic study only.[25]

In January 1992, James Perry of Detroit,

Michigan, ordered a copy of this manual and a companion book on silencers.[26] Lawrence Horn, an unemployed sound engineer, had hired Perry to murder his ex-wife and their quadriplegic eight-year-old son, Trevor. On March 3, 1993, Perry went to the home of Mildred Horn in Montgomery County, Maryland, and fatally shot her and a private duty nurse. He suffocated Trevor. Horn had wanted his ex-wife and son killed so that he could inherit a $2 million trust fund set up for the boy.[27] Both men were convicted of the killings.

A wrongful death action was filed against the publisher after it was learned that Perry had not only purchased the book but had also employed a number of the instructions in the book in carrying out the crime. The company mounted a First Amendment defense, maintaining that it had nothing to do with the triple murders. U.S. District Judge Alexander Williams Jr. dismissed the case on summary judgment, saying that the First Amendment barred the claim against the publisher. In explaining his reasoning, Williams wrote: "Admittedly, the court's task is both novel and awesome; the court must balance society's interest in compensating injured parties against the freedom of speech guaranteed by the First Amendment. The First Amendment bars the imposition of civil liability on Paladin unless *Hit Man* falls within one of the well-defined and narrowly limited classes of speech unprotected by the First Amendment."[28] The only area that

Williams found that could possibly apply was a direct incitement to imminent lawless action, but in analyzing the case under that standard, the court had to weigh "whether *Hit Man* merely advocates or teaches murder or whether it incites or encourages murder."[29] The judge looked at other cases involving television programs and movies that were alleged to have spurred violence, and he concluded, as had the judges in those cases, that *Hit Man* did not meet the incitement-to-violence standard required to override First Amendment protection. "Nothing in the book says 'go out and murder now!' Instead, the book seems to say, in so many words, 'if you want to be a hit man this is what you need to do.' This is advocacy, not incitement."[30] In sum, he told the victims' families that people kill, not words.[31]

Judge Williams's opinion is based on sound First Amendment principles, but obviously it is a difficult decision for people to understand, including some judges. The family appealed his decision. On May 7, 1997, the United States Court of Appeals heard arguments in the case in Richmond, Virginia. Conservative Judge J. Michael Luttig called the book an incitement to murder. Luttig let his feeling be known from the bench, saying he had read the book carefully and "it exhorts people to take the law into their own hands and to steel themselves to kill people."[32] Luttig was one of three judges on the panel deciding the case, and he wrote the opinion reversing the district court's ruling. On November 10, 1997, the Court of Appeals ordered that a trial be held on the issue of Paladin's account ability for murder.

This case will ultimately have an impact on whether publishers can be held accountable for how-to methods for illegal behavior. The lawsuit came at a time when Paladin was also involved in the Oklahoma bombing case for having published books on bomb making that were purchased by Timothy McVeigh. However, courts and others should not lose sight of the fact that Paladin Enterprises did not construct a bomb or carry out a murder. Holding purveyors of information accountable for how that information is used opens up a dangerous Pandora's box. Some chemistry textbooks include information on explosive chemical combinations. Should the publishers of such texts be held accountable if a depraved individual reads one of these books and concocts lethal explosives?

It is popular today to hold the messenger accountable, particularly in civil lawsuits, where recovery of large sums of money is possible. The producers of the Oliver Stone movie *Natural Born Killers* are being sued because an eighteen-year-old in Louisiana told police that she and her boyfriend took drugs and went on a killing spree after watching the movie several times. Three other teenagers killed a girl in San Luis Obispo, California, in a satanic ritual. The girl's parents are suing American Recordings because the three teens were hooked on the music of Slayer, a "death metal" band. All of these grisly situations rightly evoke emotions of sympathy for the victims and their families, but they cannot be used as a basis for casting aside First Amendment protections. If this expression loses protection, then where will courts draw the line? Crime details are presented daily in news articles and broadcasts. Would news organizations be held accountable if a depraved individual replicated what he or she read or heard in a news story?

HATE SPEECH

One of the more emotional topics involving the First Amendment in recent times — and one not likely to go away — is the discussion of how much, if any, protection should be afforded to people whose message is one of hatred or intolerance, particularly with respect to race, ethnicity, gender, national origin, religion, or sexual preference. The image problem that the First Amendment sometimes has is exacerbated by this area perhaps more than any other. People have a difficult time accepting that the Ku Klux Klan should have a right to march through town or that cross burning may be considered symbolic expression, protected by the First Amendment.

Nonetheless, the strength of the First Amendment becomes apparent through these ugly scenarios — and, in a very real sense, is fortified by them. In 1992 the Supreme Court was faced with determining if a "bias-motivated crime ordinance" in St. Paul, Minnesota, could withstand a constitutional challenge.[33] Robert A. Viktora, a St. Paul teenager, and a group of his cohorts assembled a "crudely made" cross out of broken chair legs and then burned it in the fenced-in yard of a black family living in the neighborhood. Viktora was charged under this ordinance, which provided:

> Whoever places on public or private property a symbol, object, appellation, characterization or graffiti, including, but not limited to, a burning cross or Nazi swastika, which one knows or has reasonable grounds to know arouses anger, alarm or resentment in others on the basis of race, color, creed, religion or gender commits disorderly conduct and shall be guilty of a misdemeanor.[34]

The Supreme Court ruled that the ordinance was facially unconstitutional primarily because it singled out particular areas that the St. Paul city government had found offensive. In fact, the Court found that the ordinance went "beyond mere content discrimination to actual viewpoint discrimination." Justice Antonin Scalia wrote, "The First Amendment does not permit St. Paul to impose special prohibitions on those speakers who express views on disfavored subjects."[35]

This case again illustrates the problems government runs into when it seeks to make laws based on the content of speech.

The following year the Court distinguished between those who use hate speech and those criminals who single out their victims based on race, religion, color, disability, sexual orientation, national origin, or ancestry. Wisconsin's penalty-enhancement provision was found not to be a violation of the First Amendment after Todd Mitchell had five years added to his sentence based on evidence that he severely beat a young boy walking down the street because he was a "white boy." The Court observed that its decision the previous term did not apply to the penalty-enhancement provisions and that while the ordinance in the earlier case "was explicitly directed at *expression* (i.e., 'speech' or 'messages'), the statute in this case is aimed at *conduct* unprotected by the First Amendment."[36]

Speech and conduct are separate issues, but sometimes in emotional settings one can lead quickly to the other. One area in which political expression has turned deadly is the numerous demonstrations outside abortion clinics.

A CONSTITUTIONAL LINE IN THE SAND

With groups such as Project Rescue and other right-wing religious organizations rallying behind the anti-abortion cause, the number of demonstrations outside clinics where abortions are performed has continued to rise. Demonstrations are protected under the First Amendment, but law enforcement officials have been forced to answer the troubling question of when the protected expression ends and harassment begins. Clinics have been blockaded by protesters. Cars have been surrounded by crowds.

Driving this debate is the fact that the form of these protests has, in some cases, turned violent — and even deadly in five instances. The issue garnered so much attention in the mid-1990s that Congress passed a law designed to prevent abortion protesters from blockading clinics or using force or the threat of force to prevent people from entering such clinics. In the Freedom of Access to Clinic Entrances Act,[37] Congress was careful not to completely trample the First Amendment considerations of the protesters by focusing attention on physical obstruction of clinics and the use and threat of force. Despite the act, abortion rights proponents contend that enforcement is lacking.[38] Anti-abortion demonstrators have argued that the act violates their First Amendment rights of assembly.

This is a touchy area of First Amendment law because discerning what is protected expressive activity and what goes beyond expressive activity essentially has to be handled on a case-by-case basis, which does not ordinarily add stability to the law. Nor does it offer "comfort or protection" to those marching outside such clinics. The U.S. Supreme Court has ruled that a buffer zone in front of a women's clinic restricting the location of protesters and restricting noise during normal operating hours was only an incidental limitation on free speech rights and thus not a violation of the First Amendment.[39] However, a few months later a federal court in New York struck down a court-sanctioned buffer zone at an abortion clinic in Buffalo. The court found that there was not sufficient justification for the zone to restrict the rights of the demonstrators. In a 2–1 decision, Judge Thomas J. Meskill wrote that the buffer zone keeping protesters fifteen feet away from the clinic "sweeps too broadly and burdens more of Project Rescue's constitutionally protected expression than is necessary to protect the government's significant interests in the safe performance of abortions, in public safety and in protecting all persons' constitutional rights."[40]

Then the Supreme Court weighed in with a Solomon-like decision on the buffer zone question. On February 19, 1997, the justices handed down their decision in *Schenck v. Pro-Choice Network of Western New York.* In it they reinforced the constitutionality of a fixed buffer zone, fifteen feet around the entrance to an abortion clinic, but struck down the so-called floating buffer zone fashioned by the New York court that would travel with staff members or women seeking abortions as they entered and exited the clinic. The Court felt the floating zone burdened speech more than was necessary. The floating zones were created by the New York court to stop protesters from handing out leaflets or serving as sidewalk counselors as women attempted to go into the clinics. Chief Justice William Rehnquist, writing for an 8–1 majority in this part of the opinion, said, "Leafletting and commenting on matters of public concern are classic forms of speech that lie at the heart of the First Amendment." The Court ruled 6–3 in upholding the fixed zone around the entrance, acknowledging that it was necessary to ensure public safety and allow a woman to obtain an abortion.

Just as the abortion question itself is unlikely to be resolved in the near future, if ever, the concomitant right to protest peacefully will undoubtedly remain unsettled.

The original intent and purpose of the First Amendment was to protect minority viewpoints. "Minority" often translates in this instance to "unpopular." The public's tolerance for protecting such views is waning. Curiously, the opposition to flagging the First Amendment as a safe guard to this expression comes from both sides of the American political ideology.

6

Free Expression in Cyberspace

"As the most participatory form of mass speech yet developed, the Internet deserves the highest protection from government intrusion."

— *ACLU, et al. v. Janet Reno*, 1996

On February 8, 1996, President Bill Clinton signed into law the most sweeping piece of communications legislation since the Communications Act of 1934. With occasional amendments, the Communications Act had governed all wired and wireless communications in this country for sixty-two years, taking under its wing everything from a fledgling radio industry in the 1930s to satellites and digital services in the 1990s. But industry analysts had long considered the act ineffective in governing modern communications industries.

The act's progeny, the Telecommunications Act of 1996, is considered landmark reform because it boldly changes existing law in several respects. Included in its broad sweep are regulations governing radio and television, cable, online communications, and telephone services. One of the more controversial aspects of the law is the Communications Decency Act, the provision prohibiting indecent content on the Internet. The act provides criminal penalties for those who "knowingly" transmit "indecent" communications. Within minutes after President Clinton signed the measure, a lawsuit was filed in federal court challenging its constitutional validity. Two weeks later a second lawsuit was filed by a coalition of Internet users, including publishers, news organizations, and related groups and businesses.

The lawsuit was spearheaded by a group known as the Citizen Internet Empowerment Coalition (CIEC) and was coordinated, in part, by the Center for Democracy and Technology. In announcing its challenge to the act, CIEC proclaimed that the outcome of this lawsuit "will likely determine the legal status of speech on the Internet and the future of the First Amendment in the Information Age." It is not the ability of youngsters to surf the Internet looking for pornographic materials that is at stake in the case. The critical issue is how the transmission of information over the Internet is going to be viewed in First Amendment terms.

As is often the case, the growth of technology has far surpassed the ability of the law to keep pace. And although this same scenario has been present throughout the history of all technological advancement, it is particularly significant in regard to the Internet, where growth occurs at an astonishing rate and more and more parties are involved literally every day. Almost anyone can become a publisher of material — and, in relative terms, for a nominal cost. Accordingly, the ability exists to transmit all kinds of information, viewpoints, and even tasteless, dangerous, and illegal materials. Indeed, this is happening. The question becomes how can society ensure that materials such as pornographic pictures or a recipe for a pipe bomb are kept away from those whose indiscriminate use might be harmful to themselves and others.

The law has some models through which to fashion a response to that question. The most common one is to punish those who transmit such material. It has worked, to some extent, in the past (e.g., obscenity prosecutions, fighting words, or incitement to violence). The Communications Decency Act is an attempt to rework that model to fit this new technology. Yet, the Internet is different. In order to punish the sender, the point of origin must be located. For example, in standard obscenity law, the police or other law enforcement authorities find the manufacturer — or more often the distributor (a bookstore or video rental establishment). Once the culprit is identified, an arrest can be made.

With the Internet, the point of origin is less clear and indeed can be anonymous. In fact, the material can originate outside the United States (and thus outside of U.S. laws) or it can originate domestically and then be translated anonymously outside the United States. The result is that prosecution has to be, by its very nature, selective. Moreover, it will undoubtedly be impossible to crack large crime rings trafficking in illegal materials. Add to this the difficulty in determining just what is illegal and the picture becomes clear: The First Amendment would be lost in cyberspace.

THE QUICK FIX

Congress recognized that the growth of this technology was outpacing any effort to contain the proliferation of pornography available with the click of a mouse or the stroke of a key. As the overhaul of telecommunications law occupied the front burner in Washington, Senator J. James Exon, a Democrat from Nebraska, seized the opportunity to introduce an amendment designed to punish the transmission of not just "obscene material" (which would already be prohibited under state and federal law) but also "indecent works" — expression fully protected in print, although regulable to some extent in broadcasting.

Senator Exon was successful in gaining passage of this amendment in the overall telecommunications package, although very little discussion on this provision occupied the Senate agenda. Here again, the politics of law can cloud the real issue. Most people favor keeping pornographic materials out of the hands of children. But the mechanism used by Congress to accomplish that laudable goal was constitutionally suspect from the beginning.

The Exon Amendment, as the Communications Decency Act became known, called for criminal punishment for anyone who "knowingly . . . makes, creates, or solicits . . . and initiates the transmission of any comment, request, suggestion, proposal, image, or any other communication which is obscene or indecent, knowing that the recipient of the communication is under 18 years of age."[1] The other major controversial provision made it a crime to use an "interactive computer service to . . . display in a manner available" to a minor "any comment, request, suggestion, proposal, image, or other communication that, in context, depicts or describes, in terms patently offensive as measured by contemporary community standards, sexual or excretory activities or organs, regardless of whether the user of such services placed the call or initiated the communication."[2] Critics of the law pointed out that the language encompasses too much, ranging from works of pornography to works of art. Moreover, detailed information on AIDS prevention or other sexually transmitted diseases would be verboten under these provisions. After the challenge to

169

the Communications Decency Act was filed United States District Judge Ronald L. Buckwalter issued a restraining order prohibiting enforcement of the provision until the matter was resolved in court.

JUDGES SURF THE NET

It is not very often that a group of federal judges will hover around a computer screen looking for pornographic images on the Internet. This was precisely the scene in March 1996 as the three judges made an effort to understand the technology and what comes along with it. The ceremonial courtroom on the first floor of the federal courthouse in Philadelphia provided the locale for the hearing, and it was no small accomplishment just to get the courtroom prepared. A large computer monitor was brought in and placed on a raised witness platform. High-speed phone transmission lines had to be installed as well. Additional computer monitors were placed on the judges' bench.

In addition to looking for pornography, the judges also explored the viability of blocking software — a device that parents can install on computers to keep pornographic materials off their computer screens. This software, which continues to be developed and refined, provides an alternative means of accomplishing the stated goal of the Communications Decency Act. In fact, if the true objective of the measure is to stop the reception of such materials by minors, the blocking device is a better way to achieve it, and it contains no First Amendment threat.

The Communications Decency Act itself is no guarantee that this material will be unavailable on the Internet. In fact, just as there is no practical way to stop the flow of obscene materials (not protected by the First Amendment) in print today, the same will be even more true electronically because of the enforcement difficulties mentioned earlier. Consequently, any court challenge to the act necessarily requires a balance between means least restrictive of First Amendment concerns.

The indecency prohibition sets up an unbalanced system of First Amendment rights. Under the law, to be obscene, material must be found by a judge or jury to appeal to the prurient interest, be patently offensive, and lack literary, artistic, political, or scientific value. Material not meeting that definition may be indecent. If indecent, though not legally obscene, material is presented in printed form, First Amendment protection attaches, but if that same material is posted on a World Wide Web site, the transmitter of the information can be criminally sanctioned. Such restrictions on the *content* of speech, as opposed to the time, place, or manner of the regulation, are always constitutionally suspect and must be subject to the highest level of scrutiny by the courts. The legal test, simply stated, is that a court must determine if the government has a compelling need for such restriction — and further, if the law is using the least restrictive (in terms of the First Amendment) means to accomplish the objective. Both parts of the test must be met.

In addition, when a constitutional challenge is mounted, courts are sometimes asked to determine if the language of the statute is plain and understandable or vague or overbroad. As a legal term of art, vague language is that which is ambiguous and whose meaning is not discernible from the words written. For instance, would someone reading the language used understand just what is being prohibited? In a statute that is overbroad, the reach of the law goes beyond what the drafters intended to prohibit and actually criminalizes material protected under the First Amendment.

In Judge Buckwalter's restraining order, issued in February 1996, shortly after the lawsuit was first filed, he hinted at how he might view the case on the merits later that spring. He wrote:

> First of all, I have no quarrel with the argument that Congress has a compelling interest in protecting the physical and psychological well-being of minors. Moreover, at least from the evidence before me, plaintiffs have not convinced me that Congress has failed to narrowly tailor the CDA. Where I do feel the

plaintiffs have raised serious, substantial, and doubtful questions in their argument is that the CDA is unconstitutionally vague in the use of the undefined term "indecent." This strikes me as being serious because the undefined word "indecent," standing alone, would leave reasonable people perplexed in evaluating what is or is not prohibited by the statute. It is a substantial question because this word alone is the basis for a criminal felony prosecution.[3]

HEARING IN HIGH DUDGEON

The hearing in the case lasted several weeks, with long breaks between days of testimony. On March 21, 1996, the opening day, the Citizens Internet Empowerment Coalition (CIEC) presented evidence of how the Internet works and also of how blocking software could better accomplish the government's objective. Part of the group's aim was to show the judges that the Internet can be an important research tool and that the Communications Decency Act would hurt content providers, thus lessening the breadth and depth of their offerings. In the ensuing days, the judges heard from others forecasting the negative impact of the law. Robert Croneberger, director of the Carnegie Library in Pittsburgh, testified that the term "indecency" in the CDA could even pose a threat to library card catalogs and could impose sanctions for the transmission of Shakespeare's plays.[4]

The Justice Department countered by showing that the Carnegie Library's two million entries, accessible by keywords such as "sex," could narrow a user's search without more explicit terms. Croneberger responded that even if it were feasible to label the entire on-line collection, the definitions of the terms "indecent" and "patently offensive" made it particularly difficult to do.[5]

The Justice Department's case focused on the government's need to develop a way to protect minors from exposure to harmful material. Lawyers for the government argued that the ease in accessing sexually explicit material created that need and that a speaker-based solution was viable. In other words, the burden of protecting minors falls on the message sender not the receiver. The real issue for the government was to demonstrate the pervasiveness of the Internet — in that minors could be unwittingly exposed to sexually explicit material. If that could be demonstrated, then an argument could follow for treating the Internet differently from print. In broadcast communications, for example, indecent material is regulated.[6]

In closing arguments, attorneys for the CIEC reminded the court that what so many proponents of the law, including its sponsor in addressing his Senate colleagues, waved around was material that would be considered obscene under general state and federal criminal statutes. The law long ago settled the argument of whether such obscene material falls out of the protection of the First Amendment. The driving point of this case, though, were the terms "indecent" and "patently offensive," and how content providers on the Internet would have to discern for themselves the precise meaning of that term under the law — an obviously untenable position in terms of the First Amendment.

CYBERSPEECH IS SAFE FOR NOW

The three federal judges found CIEC's arguments persuasive, and on June 11, 1996, issued a preliminary injunction against the government, prohibiting it from enforcing the terms of the Communications Decency Act. Each judge filed an opinion in support of the ruling. Chief Judge Delores Sloviter, a federal circuit judge sitting in this case, said that CIEC et al. had met the criteria for a preliminary injunction, a prime element of which is irreparable harm. "Subjecting speakers to criminal penalties for speech that is constitutionally protected in itself raises the spectre of irreparable harm," she wrote.[7] Further, she recognized that the provisions of this law would have a chilling, and not an incidental, effect on expression. Another factor a court must examine in deciding whether to issue a preliminary injunction is whether the public interest can be served by such an order. Sloviter wrote that "no long string of citations is necessary to find that the public interest weighs in favor of having access to a free flow of constitutionally protected speech."[8]

Judge Buckwalter concurred with Judge Sloviter's opinion but added his own finding that the CDA did not meet the strict scrutiny standard and was constitutionally overbroad. He further underscored his earlier belief that some of the terms were vague. To this end, he wrote: "If the government is going to intrude upon the sacred ground of the First Amendment and tell its citizens that their exercise of protected speech could land them in jail, the law imposing such a penalty must clearly define the prohibited speech not only for the potential offender but also for the potential enforcer."[9]

Judge Dalzell concurred in the opinion but differed on the vagueness question. His rationale was more basic — starting with a premise that speakers should not generally be silenced because of the content of their messages. He also subscribed to a medium-specific analysis, taking into account the unique characteristics of the technology. "The Internet is a new medium of mass communication. As such, the Supreme Court's First Amendment jurisprudence compels us to consider the special qualities of this news medium in determining whether the CDA is a constitutional exercise of governmental power," he wrote. Dalzell concluded it was not.

PICKING UP THE PIECES

Responses to the court's decision were swift. First Amendment devotees praised the decision as thorough and thoughtful — and, of course, legally sound. Advocates of the Communications Decency Act said the court's reasoning was flawed and vowed to invoke the expedited judicial review (to the Supreme Court) specified in the Telecommunications Act. On June 12, 1996, President Clinton released a statement expressing his disappointment with the decision. "I remain convinced, as I was when I signed the bill, that our Constitution allows us to help parents by enforcing this act to prevent children from being exposed to objectionable material transmitted through computer networks," he said.

The bill's main sponsor, Senator Exon, said the decision was not a setback, for he had expected as much from the three-judge panel in Philadelphia. He expressed optimism for the review at the United States Supreme Court. "From the beginning, we felt that the best chance for a considered opinion would be in the U.S. Supreme Court, and that's where the final decision will be made. Hopefully, reason and common sense will prevail in the Supreme Court."

Some of Exon's congressional colleagues did

not share his confdence. In fact, many praised the court's decision as a refusal to allow censorship. Senator Patrick Leahy (D-Vermont) called the ruling "the right decision." He said, "Let no one be confused — this is not a victory for child pornography or indecent material — but instead a victory for the First Amendment." Congressman Rick White (R-Washington) also applauded the court's finding that the CDA was unconstitutional: "Today's ruling makes the same point that we tried to make to Congress last year — if you're going to protect kids on the Internet, you have to do it in a way that protects everyone else's freedom of speech."

A few weeks after the decision, the Justice Department announced it was going to take advantage of the direct appeal provisions of the Telecommunications Act and ask the Supreme Court to hear arguments on appeal. The Court granted review and scheduled the case for October Term 1996.

ORAL ARGUMENT

A cold rain falling on Washington, D.C., did little to dampen the spirits of protesters circling the walk in front of the Supreme Court Building on March 19, 1997. Inside, lawyers for both the government and cyberpublishers prepared to argue the merits and demerits of the Communications Decency Act for the last time. The protesters came from both camps. The demonstrators could not be heard or seen from inside the courtroom, where the dignity and majesty of the nation's highest branch of the judiciary helps keep the decorum at an appropriate level.

Chief Justice William Rehnquist began by informing both sides that they would have thirty-five minutes in which to argue instead of the usual thirty. Although five minutes might not seem like a great deal to most casual observers, it can mean plenty to the lawyers who are trying to make a point amid the constant questioning of the justices. More important, it also served as a symbolic gesture that this case was somehow different — the issues at hand might be of first impression — in that the justices had not heretofore grappled with the notion of extending constitutional principles in this new medium, colloquially referred to as cyberspace.

The government's attorney, Seth Waxman, began the argument by telling the justices that all of the regulations involving indecency passed upon by the Court and all of the avenues for displaying such material — including bookstores, radio, television, cable, and telephone — do not even approach the magnitude of the "revolutionary advance in information technology" called the Internet. Waxman wanted to set the stage for convincing the justices of the critical importance of carving out new, and in effect lesser, First Amendment standards for regulating the new technology.

In the first few minutes of the argument, Waxman was interrupted by Justice Sandra Day O'Connor, who inquired about the feasibility of using CGI script, a mechanism through which Internet content providers could screen for the age of the information recipient. In other words, providers of indecent materials could ensure that viewers of their web sites were over the age of eighteen. Waxman said that there were ways around that device and that for a mere five dollars per year a minor could obtain an adult credential. The point Waxman was trying to make was that the disincentive for putting out indecent materials had to come from the criminal sanctions of the Communications Decency Act.

One hurdle the government needed to address was how this law would adversely affect those other than cyber smut peddlers. One of the parties challenging the act was the American Library Association. Libraries are going on-line in large numbers. Screening for any material that might be indecent or patently offensive would be such an onerous task for these organizations that compliance with the act would effectively make it impossible for them to continue to be players on the Internet. In fact, one of the witnesses at the district court hearing in the case had been a representative of the Carnegie Library.

In an attempt to diffuse this critical issue, Waxman hit it head-on:

Now as to the library, the Carnegie Library is an appellee in this case, and it is a very good example of what we think represents the overblown nature of the challenge to this act. The library wants to do two things. It wants to put its card catalog on-line so that anybody anywhere in the country can see what the Carnegie Library has, and it also wants to put on-line journals and abstracts that it in turn receives in an electric form. Now, the definition of what is patently offensive, that is a term of art. It is very narrow, and it is exceedingly difficult to see how it would apply to more than a handful of cards in a card catalog, but to the extent that it does, you can simply run it through some sort of word processor or computer program to screen [the material].

Waxman's oversimplification of the work involved in screening all of the information a library might have in its collection completely ignores the First Amendment ramifications of such a requirement. After all, libraries are conduits of information. Most people would readily agree that the intent of the drafters of the Communications Decency Act was not to go after libraries. Yet, under the act, libraries, schools, and universities would be held to the same standards as the pornographers for screening the content of their transmissions. The First Amendment prohibits the government from cre-

181

ating law that impinges on the free flow of information. The CDA is a complete affront to that notion. Thus, organizations such as libraries would have to determine what was meant by the terms "indecent" and "patently offensive." The law of obscenity, with its vexed set of definitions, provides ample evidence of the near impossibility of doing so. The folly of the government's logic in this case can be shown by the example that the Carnegie Library's card catalog at its facility is protected under the First Amendment but merely putting it on-line opens up the organization to federal criminal prosecution.

The other major difficulty opponents have with the Communications Decency Act is the scope of its application. The CDA encompasses not only web sites created by would-be pornographers and child predators but also E-mail, listserves, and chat rooms — the expanding usages of the Internet. E-mail provides instantaneous transmission of messages to people around the world. For instance, college students use E-mail to communicate with their friends at other institutions, their parents, and their professors. Listserves allow information to be blanketed en masse to a group of interested recipients, and chat rooms allow people to seek out like-minded individuals for discussion in real time. Justice Stephen Breyer pointed out this defect in the law in an example involving high school students.

Breyer asked the government's attorney if a

group of high school students communicating on E-mail about their sexual experiences, "real or imagined," would be subject to criminal prosecution and face two years in federal prison. Breyer made the point that E-mail, in this instance, differs hardly at all from a telephone conversation. "I even imagine high school students might read from, let's say, books or magazines that have what people might think of as patently offensive ways of describing those experiences. If you get seven high school students on a telephone call, I bet that same thing happens from time to time. And so my concern is whether, analogizing this to the telephone, it would suddenly make large numbers of high school students across the country guilty of federal crimes as they try to communicate to each other either singly or in groups," Breyer said.

Seth Waxman said nothing to alleviate Justice Breyer's concerns. In fact, he merely confirmed Breyer's reading of the act. "If high school students, like anybody else, communicate what a jury would find and what this Court would establish, given its responsibility to create a constitutional floor, to be patently offensive within the meaning of the statute, they would violate it."

Arguing on behalf of the American Civil Liberties Union and the numerous other opponents to the act, attorney Bruce Ennis made the case that the Communications Decency Act simply will not work to accomplish its own goals and that it tears at the fabric of free expression. He laid out for the Court four reasons why the CDA should fail: "The CDA bans speech. It will not be effective. There are less-restrictive alternatives that would be much more effective. And the combination of an imprecise standard, coupled with the threat of severe criminal sanctions, will chill much speech that would not be indecent." Ennis tried to help the justices understand the magnitude of their decision in aiding the free flow of information. He cited the forty million speakers who currently use news groups, listserves, and chat rooms and the technological impossibility of screening for age in those fora. Although the age-screening devices mentioned above can be employed in some, though not all, web sites, where the content is essentially just displayed, these other uses of the Internet involve interactive communication, and this interactivity is the attractive feature.

"A web site is static. What the government is saying is that the forty million people who can speak in an interactive dialogue in the other modes of communication on the Internet should post a static message on their web sites. And maybe people who are in the news group would come to see it, maybe not. But the speaker would not get any feedback. There would be no dialogue," Ennis argued.

Ennis attempted to sort out the notion of speakers in terms of commercial and noncommercial speakers. The vast majority of people who use the Internet fall into the latter category. For this category of speakers, employing the technological devices that would be needed to engage in discourse would be out of the question. They would simply be chilled out of existence on the Internet. For example, the principal way to screen for age is through the use of a credit card. Unless speakers are charging for access to their materials ("a very small subset of all Internet speakers"), most credit card companies would not do the verification. The few that would, would also charge $1 per verification. "Now if you are a speaker who wants to make your speech available to 100,000 listeners, that means you, the speaker, would have to pay $100,000 for the privilege of speaking."

Chief Justice Rehnquist was unmoved by the fact that speakers would have to pay. He likened the experience to the early radio entrepreneurs who, once regulated, had to purchase equipment to meet federal standards. Rehnquist missed the point that the early radio entrepreneurs were just that — businesspeople seeking to gain from the new technology. With the Internet, anyone — not just commercial providers — can participate in the transmission of information. Ennis picked up on the government's oversimplification of the Carnegie Library example. A word processor, as Seth Waxman argued, would not be sufficient to screen for indecent material within the meaning of the law. As Ennis told Rehnquist, "That would require a human judgment and it would cost about three million dollars to do that." Rehnquist remained unconvinced that this was problematic in terms of the First Amendment.

"I mean we do stop individual citizens from running radio stations because of all the regulations; they say it's prohibitively expensive, you can't run your own radio station. And we say, well, you know, that's tough luck. The goal to be achieved is everybody can't talk at once, so we have to limit the numbers and we have to have all of these technological requirements. It's going to cost you three million dollars, and we say that's too bad," Rehnquist said.

Ennis returned to his main argument by refocusing the Court's attention on the less-restrictive alternatives to the act. To this end, Ennis introduced the parental blocking software mentioned earlier in this chapter. Justice Souter was interested in the viability of that solution, and Ennis took advantage of the opportunity to explain about the "broad range of technologies and software programs that enable parents either completely to block all access to the Internet, if the parents are really concerned, or, more selectively, to screen and filter access to the Internet if they want to allow their children to have access to certain parts of the Internet but not to others."

The beauty of the parental blocking device is that it accomplishes what should be the goal — it keeps harmful materials away from minors.

Obviously, those in charge of the minors must exercise the option. At the same time, it does not get in the way of adult access to material. Moreover, it accomplishes the goal in a way that the act cannot. The parental blocking device keeps all indecent material off the computer screen, including material that gets into the United States from foreign transmission sites. The Communications Decency Act would be ineffective in trying to reach those providers. As Ennis pointed out to the Court, "About forty percent or more of all speech on the Internet is posted abroad in foreign countries. And at least thirty percent of all indecent speech in cyberspace is posted in foreign countries. The government's own expert acknowledged [in the district court] that the CDA would have no impact on that foreign indecent speech and that parents would have to rely on parental control technologies to shield their children from that foreign speech."

Chief Justice Rehnquist could not see the sense in that argument because the act could arguably screen out 70 percent of the indecent material, and to his way of thinking, that was an improvement. Ennis countered with an illustration from outside cyberspace: "Suppose we were talking about an enormous adult bookstore. Everything in the store is indecent. And the government says, children can come into this enormous adult bookstore and browse unsupervised, but we're going to remove half the books, half the videos. That would not, directly and materially, advance the government's interest of protecting those children from access to indecent materials."

Ennis's point is a good one. If the goal is to keep indecent material away from minors, and if the regulation cannot achieve that goal, then the regulation should fail for two reasons. First, it does not achieve the compelling interest of the government (although Chief Justice Rehnquist said in response to Ennis's example, "Well, it would certainly. It would certainly go halfway!"). Second, the parental blocking software is clearly less restrictive in terms of the First Amendment than a regulation that sweeps into its reach adult speech protected in print — and even more important, certain works of art and medical information.

The Communications Decency Act requires providers to make a judgment as to whether the material they are posting or transmitting on the Internet is indecent or patently offensive. This is an impossible task. Under the act, parents could face two years in federal prison for sending what the act might term indecent or patently offensive E-mail to their seventeen-year-old son or daughter who might be away at college. What is worse, no precise definitions of those terms are included in the act. People are left to guess what the government might declare indecent or patently offensive.

The Supreme Court agreed. On June 26,

1997, the justices released their opinion in *Reno, et al. v. American Civil Liberties Union, et al.* Instead of attempting to carve out a new standard for the Internet — one that would have created a double standard for messages in cyberspace — the Court merely applied existing First Amendment principles to the new medium. At least for now, communications over the Internet receive the same constitutional protection as the printed word. Essentially, the Court found that Congress went too far in trying to protect minors from indecent and offensive materials. Although protecting children from such harmful speech may be a critical task for the government, it does not mean that the First Amendment rights of adults should be trampled in the process:

> We are persuaded that the CDA lacks the precision that the First Amendment requires when a statute regulates the content of speech. In order to deny minors access to potentially harmful speech, the CDA effectively suppresses a large amount of speech that adults have a constitutional right to receive and to address one another. That burden on speech is unacceptable if less restrictive alternatives would be at least as effective in achieving the legitimate purpose that the statute was enacted to serve.[10]

The justices were also troubled by the vagueness of the definitions of "indecent" and "patently offensive." Picking up on a theme developed in oral argument, Justice John Paul Stevens wrote that the definitions "may also extend to discussions about prison rape or safe sexual practices, artistic images that include nude subjects, and arguably the card catalog of the Carnegie Library."[11]

Justice O'Connor and Chief Justice Rehnquist joined in a separate opinion in which they agreed that the CDA as currently framed was unconstitutional, but they said that they believed that the defects in the act were correctable. To this end, O'Connor wrote that she viewed the CDA "as little more than an attempt by Congress to create 'adult zones' on the Internet. Our precedent indicates that the creation of such zones can be constitutionally sound."[12] She went on to explain that Congress went astray because it failed to follow the "blueprint" for creating constitutional zoning laws.

O'Connor's opinion gives hope to those in Congress who plan to craft further legislation. On the day the opinion was released, Senator Patty Murray (D-Wisconsin) announced that she would introduce the Childsafe Internet Act of 1997, a plan to help keep children away from harmful material on the Internet. Murray said she would work with the White House and Internet providers on developing a ratings system for cyberspace. So far, the bill is still being developed and thus had not been introduced.

LOCAL PROBLEMS

While Congress and the Supreme Court take on the weighty issue of the First Amendment in cyberspace, states and local communities are grappling with their own set of Internet-related problems. Three states — Virginia, New York, and Georgia — have passed laws regulating Internet usage by means ranging from curbing state employees' perusal of sexually explicit sites to prohibiting pseudonyms and anonymous communications. First Amendment challenges immediately followed.

The Ohio State senate recently dropped a plan to require the Ohio Public Information Network to install content-blocking software on the state's Internet system.[13] The decision to scrap the requirement came amid a threatened challenge by the ACLU because the proposal would have required libraries to use the technology, which sometimes blocks legally permissible material. The ability of all, including minors, to access sexually explicit materials is causing headaches for libraries across the country, a majority of which are installing Internet technology. In Chicago, for example, anyone can access *Hustler* and *Penthouse* magazines in their online editions. The city's libraries follow the American Library Association view that anyone who wishes should have access.[14] This accessi-

191

bility is causing some to question why such magazines are not available in stores to minors but are made available in the local libraries. In Boston, blocking software has been installed in the children's areas of the library and in other places parental permission is required for minors to get access.

President Clinton thinks a V-chip for the Internet is the solution. He would like to see a technological solution in which a computer chip could be programmed to screen out material not appropriate for minors. As Clinton forwarded his new technology agenda, which includes wiring every public school to the Internet, he needed to explain to parents how he intended to keep schoolchildren from exposure to adult materials. On May 22, 1997, the president participated in an Internet-transmitted "town meeting" and pushed the notion that every classroom needs to be linked to the Internet by the year 2000. Although Clinton said his administration is working on a V-chip-like solution, computer experts question the feasibility of such technology when hundreds of thousands of content providers exist on the Internet.[15]

STRANGE BEDFELLOWS

As has been noted elsewhere in this book, the First Amendment cuts across political ideologies. Just as conservatives and liberals sometimes unite on First Amendment issues, they also sometimes unite in opposition to First Amendment challenges. In the area of the patrolling of cyberspace for indecent images, President Clinton, whose administration supported the Communications Decency Act and mounted the appeal to the Supreme Court, is aligned with right-wing notables such as Ralph Reed, formerly head of the Christian Coalition, and Senator Jesse Helms (R-North Carolina), who agrees with the president on little else.

Indecency is only a small part of the First Amendment picture in cyberspace. What ultimately happens to the progeny of the Communications Decency Act has less to do with pornography in terms of the law and more to do with the willingness of the courts to shape the ruling. If a separate standard is ultimately suggested or required for the Internet, the question then becomes how far can the notion of a separate standard for a specific type of speech reach. For instance, the law of defamation has some settled standards in traditional legal scenarios. Can lesser First Amendment protections exist on the Internet for material alleged to be defamatory? If so, that revelation will spell bad news for the news industry, which has already had its share of bad news these past few years in the defamation arena.

7

Ill Repute

"Under the First Amendment there is no such thing as a false idea. However pernicious an opinion may seem, we depend for its correction not on the conscience of judges and juries but on the competition of other ideas."

— *Gertz v. Robert Welch, Inc.*, 1974

It has been said that it is difficult to place a value on reputation. However, in the 1990s, juries seemed to have little trouble doing so — and in record amounts. According to figures compiled by the Libel Defense Resource Center, the average jury award in defamation actions in the first two years of the decade was $9 million. News organizations were socked with several multi-million-dollar megaverdicts. Those figures will change for the worse by the end of the decade thanks to some later cases. In the largest verdict ever, the *Wall Street Journal* was hit with a $222.7 million judgment. Until that verdict, in

March 1997, the record was held by WFAA-TV in Dallas, Texas, with its $58 million judgment. Meanwhile, a jury in Philadelphia awarded $34 million to a former public official who sued over a story in the *Philadelphia Inquirer*. Seven months later that same paper was hit with a $6 million judgment — also on the complaint of a public official.

Defamation is part of a tort law. Simply put, defamation is an injury to someone's reputation and good name. Just as the individual who is injured in an automobile accident that was someone else's fault is entitled to compensation, the law recognizes that injured reputations are compensable as well. Most of the money comprising these enormous verdicts is not meant as a direct compensation for injury. Rather, the largesse of the verdict is designed as a punishment to the wrongdoer, often a media organization, for falsely stating something scurrilous. These are called punitive damages.

The First Amendment plays a major role in most defamation cases because the tort punishes media organizations and others for their speech — and more specifically, for the content of their speech. Defamatory speech, however, does not receive the same level of First Amendment protection that other speech does. So, if an individual can prove that the statements made were indeed defamatory, that speech may lose constitutional protections depending on several other factors, most notably the status of the person or persons about whom the statement was made.

The status of the plaintiff in defamation actions is key. Is the plaintiff an ordinary private citizen or does that plaintiff possess some characteristics that move him or her into the public sphere? For example, is the plaintiff a public official? By that the law means not only elected officials but also those in government who have substantial control over the affairs of government or at least appear to the public to possess that power.[1] Perhaps the plaintiff is not connected to government but has risen to a level of notoriety in the community. In other words, people know him or her. Maybe he or she is a nationally known celebrity with access to the media, in which case he or she would be considered a public figure.[2] On the other hand, the person might essentially be a private person who voluntarily got involved in a public issue to influence the outcome one way or the other. The law views this class of plaintiffs as limited-purpose public figures.[3]

The category the plaintiff falls into is important because it determines what he or she has to prove in the case. By design, public figures have a higher standard to demonstrate because they typically have access to the media to counter the allegedly defamatory remarks. Public officials should expect "vehement, caustic, and sometimes unpleasantly sharp attacks" if public debate is to be uninhibited.[4] Private plaintiffs have a less heavy burden, and each state can decide what liability standard to require.

For public plaintiffs the standard is actual malice, a confusing term because it is unrelated to the definition of ill will, spite, or hatred usually associated with the term. To prove actual malice, the plaintiff must show that the defendant published the statement either knowing it to be false or with reckless disregard of its falsity[5] — that is, while entertaining serious doubt about the truth of the statement.[6] Actual malice must be shown by clear and convincing evidence. On the other hand, private plaintiffs in most states need only show that the defendant acted negligently — that is, carelessly or below the ordinary standard of care required in similar circumstances. Negligence can be shown by a simple preponderance of the evidence.

Another element plaintiffs must show is identification. In other words, they must prove that the statements were about them. This element does not require, however, that the statement mention a plaintiff by name. A plaintiff can satisfy this requirement by showing that persons would think of him or her when they heard the defamatory remarks. Of course, all of this is moot if the statement was never published. Technically, publication can mean transmittal to just one third party. With media defendants, this is the easiest element to show because newspapers, magazines, radio, and television have circulation and ratings data.

THE PHILADELPHIA STORY

Despite Justice William J. Brennan Jr.'s eloquent opinion in *New York Times Co. v. Sullivan*, a landmark libel case setting out wide parameters for criticizing public officials, that class of plaintiffs has faired rather well with juries in Philadelphia.

In the 1960s, Richard A. Sprague was an assistant district attorney in Philadelphia. In 1973, the *Philadelphia Inquirer* published a series of articles suggesting that Sprague had played a role in suppressing a homicide investigation involving the son of a state police official. The stories alleged that the official's son had been in the apartment of a gay man who had been murdered.[7] Sprague sued the *Inquirer* for libel, claiming that the newspaper's series had injured his reputation, and began what would become a legal battle lasting more than two decades.

At his defamation trial in 1983, Sprague was awarded $4.5 million. That judgment was overturned by an appellate court based on lack of evidence, and the *Inquirer* was granted a new trial. At the retrial, the jury again found in Sprague's favor, but this time awarded him $34 million — $2.5 million in compensatory damages and $31.5 million in punitive damages.[8] On appeal, the award was reduced, but only to $24 million. The Pennsylvania Supreme Court refused to hear the case. The *Inquirer* was considering an appeal to the United States Supreme Court, but instead settled the case for an undisclosed amount on April 1, 1996.

A second case, just months after the Sprague $34 million judgment, illustrates how juries sometimes fixate on punishing journalists with little regard for First Amendment policy considerations. This case also involved a public official — a state supreme court justice. In a May 1983 *Inquirer* series called "Above the Law," reporter Dan Biddle wrote about the judicial and extrajudicial practices of judges on the state's highest court. The Pennsylvania Supreme Court already was gaining an unfavorable reputation nationwide. In fact, in 1994 Justice Rolf Larsen was impeached after being convicted of prescription drug violations. In his series, Biddle suggested that Justice James McDermott's involvement in a case that centered on a dispute between the coal industry and the state's environmental agency raised ethical questions. The coal industry's lobbying arm was represented by a law firm that was also the largest single contributor to McDermott's campaign for the Pennsylvania Supreme Court. Moreover, McDermott had visited the coal region in a chauffeur-driven limousine provided by a partner in that firm who was also a personal friend of McDermott.[9]

Biddle also reported that Justice McDermott had intervened in his son's quest for a job as an assistant district attorney. McDermott admitted making a phone call to the district attorney, but said he made it clear that his son should get the job only if he was qualified and an opening existed. These incidents formed the core of McDermott's suit.

The jurors heard a consolidated trial. McDermott had sued for alleged defamatory statements published in the "Above the Law" series in 1983 and also for reprints of that series that were distributed at conferences and to educators. The reprints were identical to the original story, except for the addition of some editorial cartoons. The law, under a notion called "mere republication," permits separate defamation actions for each distinct publication. In its verdict the jury found that the statements made in the series published in the newspaper were not actionable. The reprints, however, were false, defamatory, and had been published with actual malice, a result so ludicrous that it could not possibly hold up on appeal, and it did not — at least until it arrived at the Pennsylvania Supreme Court.

The jury awarded McDermott the hefty sum of $6 million — $3 million in compensatory damages and $3 million in punitive damages. The compensatory damages are somewhat curious because McDermott remained on the Supreme Court until the time of his death in June 1992. The case was obviously one in which the jurors tried to check the perceived arrogance of the newspaper. In essence, though, the paper was performing the role originally intended for the press by the drafters of the First Amendment. The press was singled out in the Constitution because it needed freedom to check on government. In fact, the *Inquirer*'s attorney reminded the jurors in his closing argument that Justice McDermott had made a career decision to become a judge — a public official subject to public scrutiny. He asked them if they wanted reporters and editors to look away from wrongdoing of public officials. Unfortunately, they did not give the answer he wanted.

Although the intermediate appellate court could not justify such disparate verdicts, calling them "impermissibly inconsistent,"[10] the Pennsylvania Supreme Court had little trouble doing so. The state's highest court ruled that "there is nothing irreconcilable in its finding that McDermott failed in one instance to prove the publication false though he successfully proved falsity in the other."[11]

The *Inquirer*'s troubles just will not go away. On May 2, 1997, Milton Milan, a mayoral candidate in Camden, New Jersey, filed a defamation suit against the newspaper for stories it published on April 30 and May 1, 1997, which he claims incorrectly identified him as a suspect in a nine-year-old murder case. The newspaper has stood by the story, which included Milan's denials of involvement. The lawsuit asks for $33 million in damages. Despite the stories published in the newspaper, Milton Milan won the mayoral race.

MEGAVERDICTS IN RECORD NUMBERS

Pennsylvania juries do not stand alone in awarding enormous sums of money to libel plaintiffs. Other examples in this decade alone help support the case, and television news organizations have been among those hardest hit. In 1991, shortly after the Sprague verdict, a jury in Dallas, Texas, found against WFAA-TV in the amount of $58 million for a series of broadcasts that accused a former district attorney of taking payoffs in exchange for dropping drunk-driving cases. The verdict in this case replaced the one in the Sprague case as the largest libel judgment ever until the *Wall Street Journal* case in March 1997 (discussed below). The station's management argued that the report was fair comment on a public official, especially because the reporter began investigating the story after a federal investigation commenced, which led to the indictment of the former prosecutor.[12]

The list of megaverdicts unfortunately continues. An appellate court in Rochester, New York, upheld an $11 million libel verdict in 1995 against WKBW-TV for a story it broadcast in 1982 about a Niagara Falls restaurant owner that falsely identified him as the victim of a mob beating. With interest, the former owners of the station, Capital Cities Broadcasting, owed more than $12 million.

ABC-owned television station KGO in San Francisco was hit with a $2.5 million verdict for a 1984 series that questioned the origin and value of an antique candelabra. A wealthy Texas woman had contacted a California silversmith seeking assistance in selling this silver candelabra, which purportedly had been in the family for at least forty years. After patching some holes in the piece and attempting to sell it for nine months at a list price of $90,000, the silversmith sold it for $65,000 to the De Young Museum. The following year, KGO-TV received a tip that the candelabra had sold for too much money and might even have been stolen several years earlier. The news department did a story to this effect. The jury was convinced that the story had damaged the reputation of the silversmith and his company. The California Court of Appeal agreed.[13]

Television stations are also stinging from two major verdicts in 1996. In one case, a Texas state representative sued Houston television station KTRK for a report linking the lawmaker to a man who faked his own death in an insurance scheme. The legislator, who was in a close mayoral race at the time, lost the election. The jury awarded him more than $5 million. At the end of 1996, ABC lost a $10 million case to a Florida banker who successfully convinced a jury that a *20/20* segment had falsely accused him of misleading investors.

BREAKING THE BANK ON WALL STREET

The largest libel verdict ever also involved the investment community. On March 20, 1997, a federal court jury in Houston, Texas, handed down a $222.7 million judgment — $200 million of that figure were punitive damages against the *Wall Street Journal* and its parent company, Dow Jones, Inc. The *Journal* had published a story in 1993 about MMAR Group, Inc., a securities firm, in which reporter Laura Jereski characterized the company as reckless and freewheeling and suggested that its spending tactics might have been a factor in the loss of $50 million by the Louisiana State Employees Retirement System.[14] The company claimed it was driven out of business because of the article, though it could not prove that one client left as a result of the published story.[15]

The jury found five sentences — the costliest five sentences in American journalism — in the story to be false and defamatory. The forewoman of the jury said discrepancies among the witnesses' testimony and the reporter's finger-pointing blame on others led the jury to its decision.[16] Another juror added, "We don't want to destroy Dow Jones or the *Wall Street Journal*, but they need a little spanking, considering how much they're worth."[17]

After the trial, the judge reduced the jury's

verdict to $22.7 million, but his decision has been appealed.

A CHILLING REVELATION

Cases such as those in Houston, Philadelphia, and elsewhere are troubling, for they signal an increasing willingness on the part of the public (in the persona of a jury) and the courts to bash the media with an enormous club. Perhaps it is in retaliation for the tremendous power and influence of media institutions. Clearly, abuses run both ways. Numerous tabloid media have sullied the reputations of legitimate media everywhere. Moreover, even traditional media have found it necessary to employ some unsavory tactics or to run occasional sensational stories to compete with their tabloid counterparts. The result has been a blurring of traditional news organizations with sensationalistic infotainment programs in the eye of the public.

But slamming the media with outrageous verdicts presents a serious threat to the important role news organizations play in society and the fundamental role of the First Amendment in our public policy. The public needs the media to provide a check on government. The power the media have seized throughout history is critical to this task. No one individual, or even a group of individuals, could have exposed the Watergate scandal, an example of the use of media power for the public good. Media all over the country regularly do this type of story (although obviously not always involving the president). Readers and viewers in cities and small towns all across the country learn of public corruption, which translates most times into the improper use of tax dollars, from news organizations.

Large libel verdicts undermine the media's ability to do those types of stories. They create what Justice Brennan called in the Sullivan case a "chilling effect" on speech — not only for the companies directly hit by judgments but also for other news organizations that then question whether they ought to engage in the type of story that yielded such a huge verdict. The ripple effect of these judgments goes well beyond the borders of the coverage area of the defendant media organization. On the other hand, jurors may argue that they are simply exercising a "check and balance" on the media. In fact, because the public's opinion of media is at such a low point, it takes a tremendous leap of faith on the part of citizens to trust such profit-driven organizations to do the right thing. On balance the media, though far from perfect, provide our best hope of keeping a watch on government — a task vital to the functioning of a democracy.

Media are businesses and, as such, must make decisions based on sound business principles. If running an investigative piece translates into protracted litigation, the news organizations will have to weigh the decision to do the story about an unsavory politician or an unscrupulous business leader against the potential costs. These are precisely the stories that participants in the democracy need to know. But the costs are not just in terms of these large verdicts; most libel suits are won by media organizations on appeal, but that often takes years and tremendous amounts of money in legal costs. That is precisely where the real chill comes in — not so much from judgments. Jane E. Kirtley, executive director of the Reporters Committee for Freedom of the Press in Washington, D.C., says, "It's the prospect that you're going to have to defend against all of this that's enough to chill."

Businesses are acutely aware of this, too, according to Kirtley. "These companies are not populated by stupid people. They know that some serious saber-rattling can be sufficient to scare people off. They don't even have to file a suit. They don't even have to threaten to file a suit because people will sit around and dream up for them these various legal theories." Even more troubling to Kirtley is the growing use of torts other than libel to accomplish this same chill on the media. People who figure out that it is difficult to win a libel suit — especially on appeal — are finding solace in other causes of action, such as intentional infliction of emotional distress or invasion of privacy. "I think that the problem is not with the conventional libel suit anymore. The problem is with these companies (and I think it will inevitably include public figures) that recognize they can't win a libel suit but maybe they'll be able to sue under some other tort theory."

No one can stop someone else from filing a lawsuit, but many things can be done to discourage it. For example, potential litigants are lured by large verdicts. If a person can bash the media and collect several million dollars in the process, where is the incentive not to sue for defamation? Lawyers will likely take such a case on a contingency fee arrangement, which means that, on recovery, they will collect a percentage of the judgment (typically a third). Perhaps if the end result of the libel suit were not monetary, less incentive to sue would exist. A cap on damages in libel cases is another way to discourage some from undertaking the burden of litigation.

If, after all, the goal of any civil trial is to make the plaintiff whole, a restored reputation should be enough compensation. In the two Philadelphia cases highlighted above, the plaintiffs were not rendered destitute by the stories that ran in the newspaper. Almost a quarter of a century after the stories ran, Richard Sprague remains a successful Philadelphia trial lawyer. The late Justice James McDermott remained a vital jurist on the Supreme Court until his death. Why, then, are juries so determined to award outlandish damages in defamation cases? Such awards not only overcompensate plaintiffs but also chisel out a sizable chunk from press freedom, which, in turn, hurts all of us.

For now, though, media organizations must be willing to fight the good fight if they wish to hold on to the freedoms won in recent years. But because some large media outlets are giving in because of the costs involved, smaller organizations will not stand a chance. Jane Kirtley has seen small media outlets crushed by the costs associated with litigation: "The big, well-heeled companies have a moral obligation to fight these cases if only to deflect the fire from their smaller, less well-heeled brethren." Large media groups used to maintain a defense even for the sake of principle. For some, today, the decision is based solely on the bottom line.

Moreover, lawyers are now employed in many of the large newsrooms of the country. Although nothing is inherently wrong with having legal advice handy, surrendering control of the editorial process is detrimental to journalism. Kirtley has noticed that happens occasionally: "In some cases there is too much editorial authority being ceded to the lawyers. Obviously, it is the lawyer's job to identify whatever issues may be presented . . . but it's not the lawyer's job to basically take over the editorial decision and say this runs or doesn't run." Media lawyers typically understand that is not their role, but according to Kirtley, "they are often almost pushed into that position because management decides that the bottom-line legal issue is what's going to govern."

MIXING APPLES AND ORANGES

Keeping a watchful eye on government does not always involve uncovering corruption. Most times it means just reporting on the daily undertakings of the various branches. On occasion, reporters can spot a new bill or a court decision with important consequences for their readers or viewers. A good reporter will also take notice of a troubling trend or a related series of events. The opening pages of this book warned of the gradual, almost unnoticeable, nibbling away of free expression in this country. A classic example of this slow erosion is detectable by the traditional reporting techniques described above.

Twelve states have enacted antidisparagement laws.[18] Most people do not know about these measures and would most likely be surprised at their impact on free expression. These laws provide a legal cause of action against a person, consumer group, media organization, or other entity who makes disparaging statements about a perishable food product. They have become known as "veggie libel" bills, and although they seem so odd as to be humorous, they present a very real First Amendment threat to the flow of important consumer information.

Such bills are born of the Alar incident in the late 1980s. At the time, numerous stories appearing in the media warned consumers about the application of Alar to Washington State apples to prolong their shelf life. This chemical preservative was controversial and considered by some in the scientific community to be a cancer-causing agent. (Some scientific studies later disputed the claims of linkages between Alar and cancer.) Apple growers reported losses in the millions of dollars associated with these warnings in the media. The jolt to the economy in that state has served as the "poster child" to other states considering such bills. California, Maryland, Nebraska, Pennsylvania, Vermont, and Wisconsin have all considered bills. The Western Growers Association vowed to raise an antidisparagement bill in the California legislature every year until it becomes law.[19]

It is understandable for states to wish to protect their agricultural products, but consumers also need information to make intelligent choices when it comes to food they bring into their households. If a particular pesticide has health risks associated with it, consumer groups and media should freely pass along that information and let consumers make their own choices. Antidisparagement laws loom as an ever-present "chill" to free expression. News organizations and consumer groups will have to consider carefully whether to inform their audiences in states where antidisparagement laws exist. The Reporters Committee's Jane Kirtley calls these laws disturbing: "This is not a theoretical risk. It is very real, and I think it's just that nobody's tested it yet. But it'll come. It'll happen. The first time somebody writes a story about how cantaloupes are a great medium for salmonella and you'd better not eat them on a salad bar, there's going to be a lawsuit." To some, particularly growers and pesticide companies — the chief lobbyists in favor of these laws — making these groups think twice before publishing something is a desirable effect, but no one can logically argue that the First Amendment does not suffer as a result of these measures.

Perhaps the most notorious test of these anti-disparagement laws will come not from growers but from Texas cattlemen. Paul Engler, an Amarillo cattle feeder, is leading a group of a dozen other ranchers in a lawsuit against talk show host Oprah Winfrey and a guest on her program who claimed that feeding animal parts to cattle could spread mad cow disease to humans in this country. Winfrey swore off hamburgers on that show, and cattle prices dropped. The cattlemen are using the Texas agricultural products ("veggie libel") law as the basis for the lawsuit in federal court.

A MATTER OF OPINION

In ordinary parlance, Americans have long recognized a distinction between stating facts and giving opinions. Junior and senior high school students are typically reminded of the distinction in their English classes or debate clubs and carry it with them throughout adult life. Though most times we ascribe more value to fact than to opinion, we also relish opinion and recognize it for its own intrinsic value. Almost every newspaper in the country has an opinion page, radio and television stations regularly do commentary, and talk radio and pundit-filled television shows could not survive without opinion. People read books, watch movies, and go to the theater based on reviews they have read.

A legal reason for exalting opinion once existed. For the law was more tolerant of opinion, and from about 1974 to 1990, libel cases based on opinion were all but sure losers for the plaintiffs. The reason was simple, and those dates are significant. In 1974, in writing the Supreme Court's decision in *Gertz v. Robert Welch, Inc.*, Justice Lewis F. Powell included a passage that would for the next sixteen years serve as essentially a rule of law. Powell wrote: "Under the First Amendment there is no such thing as a false idea. However pernicious an opinion may seem, we depend for its correction not on the conscience of judges and juries but on the competition of other ideas."[20] Lower courts ran with that notion, which assisted with the disposition of numerous libel cases across the country. It also provided a welcome sigh of relief to editorial and op-ed writers, columnists, and reviewers. Having what was essentially an immunity does wonders for free expression. But that free spirit abruptly ended in 1990, when the Court handed down its opinion in *Milkovich v. Lorain Journal Co.*[21]

The Milkovich case was another example of marathon defamation litigation — this one lasted fifteen years. It all began when Theodore Diadiun, a sports columnist for the *News-Herald*, wrote about a wrestling match that turned ugly at Maple Heights High School in Maple Heights, Ohio. The state school athletic association held a hearing to investigate a fight that had broken out at the match. Wrestling coach Mike Milkovich and Maple Heights school superintendent Don Scott testified at the hearing, and again in court.

Diadiun attended the hearings, and his regular sports column, called "TD Says," carried the headline MAPLE BEAT THE LAW WITH THE BIG LIE. The headline on the jump page of the column was DIADIUN SAYS MAPLE TOLD A LIE. In the column Diadiun asserted that the coach and the superintendent were not forthright with the school association officials. To this end, he wrote:

Anyone who attended the meet, whether he be from Maple Heights, Mentor [the opposing school] or impartial observer, knows in his heart that Milkovich and Scott lied at the hearing after each having given his solemn oath to tell the truth. But they got away with it.[22]

214

The column went on to question if this was the type of lesson schools should be teaching their young people. Milkovich sued the newspaper, claiming that the passage quoted above, considered along with the head-lines, imputed upon him the crime of perjury and thus was libelous. The case proceeded through the appellate courts in a circuitous pattern, and eventually landed at the United States Supreme Court. The Ohio Supreme Court had ruled in the newspaper's favor, saying, "Even the most gullible reader" recognized that the sports page was a "traditional haven for cajoling, invective, and hyperbole."[23]

Lawyers for the newspaper tried to rely on Powell's passage from the *Gertz* decision and on subsequent lower court case law to argue that opinions are not actionable. This column was Diadiun's opinion. Under previous law interpreting Justice Powell's language in *Gertz*, only statement fact was actionable. One court had even developed a four-part test designed to help differentiate between fact and opinion.[24] Columnists give their opinions, plain and simple. But it was not so plain nor was it simple for the Supreme Court. The Court refused to ratify the notion that opinion was never actionable. In fact, it refuted the argument that Powell's language suggested such: "Thus, we do not think this passage from *Gertz* was intended to create a wholesale defamation exemption for anything that might be labeled 'opinion.' "[25]

The Supreme Court essentially cast aside an immunity for opinion that had, in application, existed since 1974. It also notified people who did not care for a review of their particular restaurant, theater production, movie, or book that opinion is not sacrosanct, and it can form the basis for a libel suit. If we accept the notion that the First Amendment is a good thing, that we all benefit from a free press, then the *Milkovich* decision runs counter to our democratic ideals in the United States. Americans long ago embraced the idea that a free press is vital to our form of government. It is no coincidence that it is called "the Fourth Estate."

What decisions like *Milkovich* do is open up huge possibilities for people to sue. That is precisely what happened shortly after the Supreme Court's decision. Dan Moldea, an author based in Washington, D.C., filed a libel lawsuit against the New York Times Company for an unfavorable review of his book *Interference: How Organized Crime Influences Professional Football.* The suit alleged that a review by a *Times* sportswriter falsely portrayed him as a "sloppy and incompetent journalist." Moldea was quoted as calling the *Milkovich* ruling a "godsend" for his case.

Moldea eventually lost his suit against the New York Times Company, but the litigation lasted five years. The expense associated with defending such a protracted case is astronomical and truly unfortunate in terms of the First Amendment's freedom of the press. Five years of legal expenses just for calling an author "sloppy" in a review (clearly understood as opinion). Perhaps the *New York Times* can afford such a costly fight (although it should not have to), but most of the country's newspapers are small, community organizations.

Post-*Milkovich*, those who render opinions must take care to ensure that they do not imply an underlying false assertion; that is, the underlying facts are incorrect, incomplete, or the basis of an erroneous assessment. In other words, pure opinion (something not provably false) is still granted First Amendment protection. Nonetheless, the "chill" on speakers may not be in the eventual verdict in court. Rather, it lies in the costly process along the way.

A REFORMATION OF SORTS

The topic of libel reform is not a new one. For many years, legal scholars and practitioners have rallied the cause of reforming the nation's defamation's laws. If truth be told, the laws have changed with Supreme Court decisions over the years, but legislative reform of libel must necessarily take place on a state-by-state basis. Of course, each state is now free to develop its own libel law, provided it takes into account the Supreme Court pronouncements. Attempts to make laws essentially uniform among the states have been successful in the past. For example, the Uniform Commercial Code has been adopted in almost every state. This uniformity makes it easier for companies to conduct business in several states. An attempt to accomplish something similar with respect to defamation law is currently in progress, although the prognosis is not good.

Several attempts at creating a uniform defamation law have gone unheralded over the years. The most recent approach is a more modest version. Predictably, plaintiff attorneys are strident in their objections to such laws, for they would clearly mean a substantial diminution of monetary damages (and, of course, attorneys' fees). On the other hand, the media are also leery about relinquishing any control over the content of their publications. In 1993, the National Conference of Commissioners on Uniform State Laws released its proposal, the "Uniform Correction or Clarification of Defamation Act." Media organizations have supported the watered-down version, but some see it as a law favoring the institutional ownership more so than the reporters in the trenches. Jane Kirtley, whose group champions the rights of reporters, is just such a critic. Kirtley explained her reasoning this way:

There are two things specifically that cause me concern. One thing is that there is an escape clause where you can get out of one of these cases if you argue that you were not publishing the disputed statement supporting the truth of it — that you were simply publishing it because somebody else said it and you thought it was of news value. The catch to it is that if you do that, you have to identify who said it, which seems perfectly logical. But what that tells me is that if somebody's real purpose is to find out who the leaker was . . . the threat of a libel suit and this kind of process will be the clever way to smoke out the information you wouldn't be able to get otherwise.

The other problem Kirtley sees with the legislation is the incentive for management to "hang reporters out to dry" in that a suit can be avoided by publishing a correction. She finds this especially to be true where a reporter has since moved on to another publication or media outlet. The media organization being sued will not feel any obligation toward its former employee and will issue a statement saying the reporter erred. That may serve the media organization's immediate purpose, but the reporter's reputation suffers.

The *Philadelphia Inquirer* was able to use an alternative resolution to avoid a libel suit in 1996. On April 18 and 19, 1996, the newspaper published articles claiming that Philadelphia's ex-police chief Willie L. Williams had had knowledge of a sting operation aimed at four officers but nonetheless transferred the officers to new assignments, and that now he was under investigation. On May 8, 1996, Williams, who had by this time become the police chief of Los Angeles, demanded through his attorneys that the newspaper retract the statements. The *Inquirer* rechecked its sources and indeed discovered that they did not have direct knowledge that the police chief had been briefed in advance of the transfer.

Working with the California retraction statute, the newspaper and Williams resolved the dispute by having the *Inquirer* publish a front-page story acknowledging the inaccuracy of the earlier articles. The position of the story and the point size of the headline were similar to those of the original articles; the headline read EX-CHIEF WILLIAMS IS NOT A SUBJECT OF INVESTIGATION.

Under the Uniform Act, a person would not be able to maintain a defamation action if "the person has made a timely and adequate request for correction or clarification from the defendant or the defendant has made a correction or clarification."[26] If the correction or clarification was made in a timely manner, the person suing would be able to collect only "provable economic loss, as mitigated by the correction or clarification."[27] Despite the reduction of damages and, in some cases, avoidance of trial, the Uniform Act is unlikely to become law in many states. Trial lawyers typically oppose the legislation — and the reasons are obvious.

ETHICS AND THE FIRST AMENDMENT

Lately the media have found themselves in some unflattering poses, something that continues to tarnish their image in the public's mind. As has been demonstrated throughout this chapter, the media's poor reputation now too often translates into large verdicts. Sometimes the media tread close to the First Amendment line of demarcation, and although they may not cross it, they come perilously close to doing so and thus suffer as much image damage when the public questions their ethics.

Perhaps the most stark example is the media's coverage of Richard Jewell in connection with the 1996 bombing at the Olympic Park in Atlanta. Jewell, a thirty-four-year-old law enforcement wannabe, was between jobs when he took a temporary security position at the Summer Olympics. On Friday night, July 27, 1996, Jewell spotted a suspicious package at the heavily occupied park. Through his efforts, several lives were saved that night, although one person died at the site after the bomb exploded and more than one hundred others were injured. But in three short days Jewell went from hero to suspect, and soon the media's eyes and cameras were trained on the Atlanta security guard. In the month that followed, Jewell's private life was transformed into a public spectacle, until the

FBI announced that he was no longer a suspect. During that month the news media, in hurried fashion, publicly sorted through the details of the investigation of this young man, who, in the final analysis, was never charged.

What happened to Richard Jewell will for some time be debated at professional and academic conferences on media ethics, but the litigation arising out of the incident may do some serious damage to the First Amendment. L. Lin Wood, an Atlanta attorney, is the lead counsel for Richard Jewell in several lawsuits against media organizations. His legal strategy naturally has encompassed the public's growing intolerance for the media. "I think we have moved away from that trust the public once had in the media — the trust that's so important because the media's there to inform us. And when we trust the media to inform us and they let us down, they breach that trust," he noted. Lin added that the breakdown of trust leads to cynicism and the widening gap between the way the media is perceived by the public and the way in which they would like to be perceived.

The way in which the story was reported rankled Jewell's lawyer in some unsettling ways. "It was not that he was a suspect. Reporting that — while we might question the ethics, we would not question the legality — but it was the portrayal by the media that Richard Jewell was, in some fashion, an aberrant personality or bizarre person who was most likely the bomber." Wood believes that within a short period of time, the public began to realize that Jewell was a "victim." They considered what they were reading, watching, and hearing and "look[ed] at Richard Jewell with more credibility than they viewed the media."

According to Wood, the media's rush to judgment included not only the traditional broadcast and print media but also the new forms of media, such as the Internet: "A number of articles published by the various organizations on the World Wide Web, we believe, contain defamatory information about Richard Jewell." Wood is continuing to research those sites with the aim of filing lawsuits against these organizations. In one of the cases, which already has been resolved, the claim included allegations of damages arising out of articles published on CNN Interactive, the news network's web site. Consequently, the question of the scope of First Amendment protection in cyberspace will probably be played out in the near future.

The First Amendment consequences will likely arise not from changes in the existing law but from the use of nontraditional law to skirt established First Amendment doctrine. Although the classic illustration of this tactic came to fruition in the Food Lion case (discussed below), Wood has included it in his own strategy.

We've looked at the traditional causes of action. In Georgia, we call television defamation "defamacast." We obviously had defamacast in terms of the television reporting. We had the classic libel in terms of the newspaper reports. We have slander with respect to the individuals connected with Piedmont College [where Jewell worked in campus law enforcement] who were quoted around the country — speaking about Richard in terms that were both false and defamatory. And, then, of course, we have obviously the invasion of privacy which is somewhat unique in this situation in terms of the media's twenty-four-hour surveillance of Richard and his mother for that first month after the bombing.

The surveillance issue presents an opportunity to direct attention away from the First Amendment defenses readily available in defamation cases. The theory Wood is advancing is Jewell's and his mother's right to seclusion — in essence, the right to be left alone. According to Wood, the invasion of privacy "is based on the fact that, for approximately one month, the media had the pool camera, which was trained on Richard Jewell's mother's apartment for twenty-four hours a day, and a media pool surveillance car which followed Richard Jewell everywhere that he went. In Georgia, we recognize a right to seclusion as part of the right of privacy, and we believe that early on after the FBI search, it should have been readily apparent that there was no reasonable belief that there was going to be an imminent arrest of Richard Jewell." Wood also asserted that, despite this, the camera and the car remained for thirty days without any news-worthy event.

Wood said he was troubled by the media's inaccuracy with respect to the reporting on his client. The media acted in great haste to get information without paying attention to getting the story correctly. The Atlanta lawyer said the law should change to provide disincentives to this type of reporting. "I even advocate that there should be strict liability in the situation where [the media identify] a suspect early in the investigation and then report false information about that person," he mused.

Strict liability is a legal concept seen most fre-quently in products liability cases, in which a manufacturer is held liable if it sells defective products. In such cases it is not necessary to show the intent of the wrongdoer — selling the product is enough. In a media situation, Wood advocated that if the media printed false infor-mation, they are liable without having to prove any legal fault such as negligence or actual malice — publishing the false information is enough. Such a notion flies in the face of current libel law and the First Amendment generally. Nevertheless, Wood likely could find support for his views, especially from a public that has grown tired of the media's perceived arrogance.

Another way to make the point is to escape traditional First Amendment doctrine by, as Wood will do with the seclusion cause of action, giving the jury alternative ways of finding a remedy for the aggrieved party. A jury in Greensboro, North Carolina, did so in ways that will continue to have a far-reaching First Amendment fallout.

THE LION ROARS

The media have not fared well in recent court battles, and, like Richard Jewell's attorney, many lawyers have found creative ways to get the news-gathering process under a juried microscope. Perhaps the sharpest example of this tactic has been the case in which the Food Lion supermarket chain sued ABC News for a story it ran on the television show *Prime Time Live*. On January 22, 1997, a federal jury in Greensboro, North Carolina, ordered ABC to pay $5.5 million in punitive damages to the supermarket chain. The judge later reduced the figure to $315,000. At issue in the case was not the truth or falsity of the story (as would be the case in an ordinary defamation suit), and, in fact, the judge instructed the jury to assume the story was true. Instead, the issue in the case was whether ABC's tactics in reporting the story, which included having producers pose as supermarket workers, lying on job applications to get positions in the store, and using hidden cameras to record what took place once inside, constituted violations of civil law.

The story ABC was pursuing was an important one. In 1992, *Prime Time Live* aired a report about unsanitary food handling by Food Lion workers. That report included interviews with former Food Lion employees, who corroborated the report of unsafe practices; it also included footage gathered by ABC's journalists, who documented Food Lion employees' repackaging spoiled meat and putting it out for sale. The case, however, focused not on Food Lion's practices but on ABC's practices. The supermarket chain's lawyers had strategically decided not to file a defamation case because all of the time-honored defamation defenses would have come into play. Also, the supermarket would have had to prove the story false. Instead, they sued the network for fraud, trespass, and breach of employee loyalty — arguing successfully that the undercover reporters should have prevented the sale of the spoiled products.

The case has set off a debate on news-gathering practices throughout the media industries. The ethicists have weighed in with various concerns, including whether it is ever appropriate for a journalist to lie to get a story. In the Food Lion case, the undercover journalists lied to Food Lion on the employment applications. Journalists, after all, are supposed to pursue the truth. Do the ends — exposing unsanitary practices — justify the means — deception? Lying clearly does weaken a journalist's credibility and should not be taken lightly, but it is unlikely that powerful footage of catching people in the act of wrongdoing could ever be gathered if reporters walked in with cameras in sight and rolling. The public needs to judge for itself whether it wants to know about unsafe food handling or abuse in day care and nursing homes enough to accept some deception in the act of news gathering. The public in Greensboro gave ABC an answer.

THE PUBLIC'S RIGHT TO KNOW

For many years the media have been able to rely on the notion that they are, in effect, surrogates for the public. And that the public has a right to know certain information, particularly when it affects their safety or the spending of their tax dollars. This latter concept is particularly crucial in a democracy. As the eyes and ears of the public, the media should report information it gathers, but drawing the line between what the public has a right to know or should know and what should be kept quiet to protect an individual's privacy has never been adequately resolved. People often can reach a general sense of agreement that victims of crime should enjoy a degree of privacy, but criminal suspects are less likely to engender the same level of sympathy — at least they were until the Richard Jewell case.

Jewell's attorney, L. Lin Wood, has argued

that the public should be concerned with the release of information about a suspect because "once [the media] identified [an individual] as a suspect, [they] have prejudiced him or her. Then if [they] go further and begin to publish false information about that person, [they] are taking a suspect in the public's mind and pushing them more toward being guilty of a crime, and that person, like Richard Jewell, may never, in fact, be charged because there was never any legitimate evidence that tied Richard Jewell to this crime in any fashion." The tension between the news-gathering process and the orderly functioning of the criminal justice system is an endemic problem. Wood said it would have been impossible for Richard Jewell to have received a fair trial had he been charged with a crime because the coverage was worldwide in scope. "The legal system obviously cannot intervene at a stage where the damage can be done," Wood suggested. "No judge can prohibit newspaper coverage on a story that is, in effect, yet to get into the courtroom." He does recommend, however, that once charges are brought, a balancing must take place between the public's right to know and the defendant's right to a fair trial.

Wood is adamant that the media should police themselves with respect to releasing a suspect's name, and touting the public's right to know just does not pass muster anymore. In the Jewell case, he said, the FBI's "evidence" was "nonexistent." Accordingly, Jewell should never have surfaced as a suspect. "I also look at it from the standpoint of why did the public need to know the name Richard Jewell in terms of being a suspect. What was the public's need to know? I can't find any reason. Richard was obviously being interviewed to a certain extent as a hero, as a person who had, in fact, been directly involved in trying to prevent the bombing or lessen its impact, but there was plenty of time to write about Richard Jewell if [the FBI] had ever found any evidence against him. All they had to do is wait. If [the media] had waited just a few days, they would not have written those stories because they would have learned that there was not going to be an arrest because there was probably not going to be any evidence against Richard Jewell."

Wood really does not expect the Jewell case to have any profound change on the way journalists operate. "The media [are] driven in the final analysis by profits. The competition is intense, and it's a world of instant communication. So the emphasis is going to remain on getting it first as opposed to the old maxim of get it first but get it right," he said.

Although libel reform could lessen the media's litigation expenses, it is unlikely to enjoy widespread adoption. Moreover, the libel issues examined in this chapter are symptomatic of a larger problem of the unpopularity of the news media today. Jurors have little difficulty in assessing large judgments against media organizations. By doing so, they are perhaps unwittingly contributing to a deterioration of the First Amendment principles embodied in the notion of unfettered debate. Public officials are winning many of these libel suits, at least at the trial level. If news organizations can no longer feel risk-free in commenting on how public officials do their jobs, then the watchdog relationship of media to government is in serious trouble.

Lawyers have found their way around the First Amendment with creative causes of action that are not subject to long-settled defenses. This poses a serious threat to free expression because the result is quite different — punishing news organizations not because their stories were false and defamatory but because the way they got the stories was suspect. The jury verdicts in these cases send a strong message, one that will likely chill investigative reporting to some extent. News organizations will claim that they will continue to report on important stories, but this bravado does not replace the fact that news management in small and large markets alike will hesitate before pursuing a controversial piece, and in some cases that pursuit will be dropped because the outcome is too risky.

In some ways, the megaverdicts in defamation cases — which bring a certain chill — although troubling, are less so than the legal tactics in the Food Lion case. At least in defamation the First Amendment remains a tool, albeit a weakened one.

8

Government and the Arts

"Paintings, photographs, prints, and sculpture . . . always communicate some idea or concept to those who view it, and as such are entitled to First Amendment protection."

— *Lederman v. City of New York*, 1996

The last entity one should expect to be an arts and entertainment critic is the federal government. In the 1990s not only the federal government but also state and local governments ventured into that critical thicket — with some murky consequences for the First Amendment. Topping off the decade were two high-profile incidents involving the government's subjective judgment on the artistic value of a particular work. A photographic exhibition of the work of the late homoerotic artist Robert Mapplethorpe was barred from opening at the Corcoran Gallery in Washington, D.C. When that same exhibit opened in Cincinnati, it resulted in the arrest of museum officials and their trial on obscenity charges. In Florida, the Miami-based rap group 2 Live Crew faced criminal charges for the live performance of its song titled "As Nasty As They Wanna Be." A federal judge there had declared the song to be off-limits — again, for its obscene content.

These events set the stage for a lingering debate over just how much influence the government should have in determining what is art and entertainment and what is criminally actionable. The Mapplethorpe controversy further fueled the debate over federal funding for the arts. If the government is going to give a boost to artists to ensure a diversity in the type of arts Americans experience does it have the concomitant right to decide which art gets funded based on a set of moral values put together by Congress or some other government entity? The artistic community clearly answers that question in the negative, but some members of Congress, including the outspoken Senator Jesse Helms (R-North Carolina), have strongly advocated government control. He is joined by a chorus, albeit a minority, of vociferous supporters nationwide who have promoted the cause of censorship in the arts — although they do not typically phrase it that way.

A moral force in society is more than hinting at government control over what Americans receive in terms of art and entertainment. Clearly, the government is taking full advantage of a national discourse on family values, no matter how ill-defined the term is.

POLITICS AND THE ARTS

A rumble of volcanic proportions rocked its way through Washington, D.C., in the early part of this decade over the propriety of federally funded art projects. Providing such funding had generally been seen as a good idea until Robert Mapplethorpe's photo exhibition and Andres Serrano's picture of an upside-down crucifix submerged in urine received endowment monies. Funds are provided through the National Endowment for the Arts (NEA), a congressionally created agency promoting the arts in the United States. These projects raised the ire of a number of conservative representatives, most particularly North Carolina's Senator Helms.

Conservative lawmakers have been successful in cutting several million dollars from the NEA's budget during the 1990s, although closing it down completely was the preferred course of action for some. The controversy was made more interesting by the politics of the Bush administration on the issue in 1990. Senator Helms had launched a campaign to place tighter restrictions on the types of projects the NEA could fund. The restrictions were content-based and were designed to weed out works that some conservatives thought to be morally reprehensible. On the firing line at the time was the chairman of the National Endowment, John E. Frohnmeyer. While conservative lawmakers were turning up the heat on Frohnmeyer in congressional hearings, the Bush administration publicly backed him and opposed the proposed restrictions on the content of art supported with federal monies.

The Bush administration's refusal to go along with content restrictions angered the social and religious right. Although supporters of the arts praised the Bush administration for its courage to back up free expression and claimed the protests were coming from a minority of right-wing zealots, the highly public debate clearly cost the administration some key support as it headed into the 1992 reelection campaign.

Moreover, the conservatives in Congress did not relent. Restrictions on federal monies were put in place, and the NEA was forced to deny applications by artists whose work could be construed as obscene. Frohnmeyer continued to be outspoken on the funding issue, opposing content-based restrictions but reluctantly agreeing to enforce them. Artists also had to sign a promissory letter saying they would obey the ban on obscene work.[1]

The battle cry in Washington became louder, and the heat on the Bush administration by religious conservatives resulted in an attitude change at the White House, particularly as the election grew nearer. By 1992, conservative commentator and Bush presidential challenger

Patrick Buchanan had made several attacks on the president for increasing support of the arts endowment, what Buchanan termed "the upholstered playpen of the arts and crafts auxiliary of the Eastern liberal establishment."[2] As a result of the magnitude of the attacks, Bush could no longer afford politically to support Frohnmeyer, whom he had ardently defended on many occasions. When Bush learned of Buchanan's plans to make an issue out of Bush's support for the arts while campaigning in conservative southern states, Bush called for Frohnmeyer's resignation.

Of course, Frohnmeyer's departure (which he chronicled in a book, aptly titled *Leaving Town Alive*) did not end the controversy over federally funded art projects. In fact, a group of artists whose application for NEA funds was denied filed a lawsuit against the government, claiming that the governing statute that sets forth the standard for funding approval violated the First and Fifth Amendments to the Constitution. The artists alleged that the requirements are content-based restrictions on speech and should be void for vagueness. The provision at issue required the NEA to "tak[e] into consideration general standards of decency and respect for the diverse beliefs and values of the American public."[3] The United States District Court agreed with the artists.[4] On appeal, the United States Court of Appeals for the Ninth Circuit rejected the NEA's argument that the "decency and respect" standard was not an issue. To the contrary, the Ninth Circuit wrote in its opinion upholding the district court's ruling: "The 'decency and respect' provision was enacted to prevent the funding of particular types of art. To that end, it places a mandatory duty on the chairperson to ensure that grant applications are judged according to 'general standards of decency and respect. . . .' The chairperson has no discretion to ignore this obligation, enforce only a part of it, or give it a cramped construction."[5] Accordingly, a First Amendment restoration of sorts has come back to federally funded arts projects, at least for now, and those inside the world of the arts would like to keep it that way.

STAR POWER BROKERS

On Monday, March 10, 1997, the artistic world celebrated Arts Advocacy Day and marked the celebration with a special lobbying effort on Capitol Hill. Coming out for the day was actor Alec Baldwin, who described himself as "president of the Creative Coalition, a New York-based group of entertainment industry professionals involved in arts advocacy and other issues, a member of the board of People for the American Way, an actor, a taxpayer, a father, a lover of the arts, and a lover of freedom." He was in Washington in all those capacities to persuade members of Congress that the arts are a good investment for America.

The effort was organized by People for the American Way on behalf of many local communities that depend on federal funding to bring the arts to places that otherwise would not have such exposure. The theme that Baldwin brought with him was "Vote Smart, Support the Arts." The group, according to Baldwin, hoped to influence a series of votes in Congress on "reauthorization and funding of the National Endowment for the Arts, on support for quality education, which by definition includes the arts at its core, on wrongheaded efforts to restrict the freedom of nonprofit organizations to speak out on public policy."

At a press conference held at the National Press Club, Baldwin criticized a quote by David Boaz of the Cato Institute who said, in opposing refunding of the NEA, that "government should stay out of arts and ideas." Baldwin said that a nation should define itself "by our commitment to our cultural heritage, to the arts, and to ideas." He noted that indeed people look to the United States as a leader in expressive freedom: "To many Americans and to people around the world, the United States is defined precisely by the ideas embodied in our government. Fundamental freedoms of religion and speech, the idea that individual liberties are not subject to the will of the majority or the passing prejudices of a given day." The government must safeguard those liberties, according to Baldwin, if the nation is to prosper.

The actor, known best for his films, has worked to spread the message that protection of the arts through our constitutional liberties is a democratic ideal. Baldwin's mission was to make clear that arts funding helps promote the education of our country's citizens, yet the United States is behind the curve on such funding. "Germany and France, Italy, Great Britain and Spain, and many other countries that are both our political allies and our economic competitors devote vastly more of their public resources to support for the arts," Baldwin said.

Baldwin also pointed out that for some three decades partisan politics played no major role in arts funding. The NEA "flourished" under Richard Nixon. Yet, in very recent times, "petty politics" has overshadowed the issue. Opponents of arts funding are quick to use red herrings to divert public attention, Baldwin said, noting that "some politicians and political groups have decided to hold up for ridicule a few artists and a few works of art, and they have tried to use that ridicule to diminish public support for the arts as a whole." The actor called this tactic a "profoundly disingenuous campaign of misinformation and myth making." He added that accessibility to the arts beyond the nation's major urban centers is a central focus of arts funding. Those federal dollars are often leveraged on the state level and in the private sector to bring more support for the arts. This point is often lost in the rhetoric of casting arts funding as welfare for the elite — or, worse yet, encouragement for pornographers. Baldwin characterized this latter argument as "enemies of arts funding [rolling] out a handful of tired old examples of controversial projects in order to tarnish the image of the overwhelmingly successful NEA that has administered over 120,000 grants in this country." Baldwin concedes that perfection is not found in any area of government, including the NEA, and that "unrestricted constitutionally guaranteed freedom of expression sometimes and rarely results in objectionable material."

Nonetheless, pornography is not the goal of NEA grants, even though, as Baldwin acknowledged, opponents of arts funding make a great effort to present this as the case:

> Each session of Congress, conservative and fundamentalist religious forces unite in an effort to scour the index of the NEA's recent grants in an effort to unearth more ammunition for their war on arts funding. This year that mantle is being carried by Republican Congressman Peter Hoekstra of Michigan. Mr. Hoekstra, in an effort to expose government waste, himself wasted vast sums of congressional and NEA man-hours in order to uncover a grant recipient called "Women

Make Movies." After doggedly researching the catalog of "Women Make Movies," he came upon a film titled *Watermelon Woman*. Hoekstra presumably viewed the film and demonized its casual depictions of drug use and sex. The central characters in the film are African-American women and are lesbians, which feeds directly into the anti-NEA's classic witch-hunt strategy of intolerant attacks on less-powerful political forces in our country — women, Blacks, homosexuals.

Baldwin also made the point that the arts make good economic sense for the government. He noted that the arts contribute $36.8 billion to the U.S. economy and employ some 1.3 million Americans, with a total payroll of $25 billion. That payroll generates $3.4 billion in federal income taxes. Those figures compare to the $99.5 million that the federal government spent on the National Endowment for the Arts in the 1996–97 budget.

The actor, along with fellow performers Marlo Thomas and Brenda Boozer, carried this message to Capitol Hill and found a warm reception from some unlikely people. House Speaker Newt Gingrich talked with the contingent, in an unscheduled meeting, after Republican congressional supporter Mark Foley of Florida made a phone call to the Speaker.[6]

Alec Baldwin lamented that the votes to once again fund the NEA are there in Congress but

241

the leadership is stalling. Over the past few years, the actor said, arts advocacy groups have been effective in getting the attention of moderate and even some conservative Republicans and convincing them that arts funding is a good thing. Baldwin was quick to point out that arts education in the schools helps students perform well on standardized tests: "According to the College Entrance Examination Board, students with four years of arts studies scored 53 points higher on the verbal and 35 points higher on the math portion of the SAT than those with no arts education."

But perhaps the one area in which arts groups are able best to catch the interest of lawmakers is by directing attention to the views of their constituents. Baldwin noted that it is a myth that the general public does not support arts funding. "Conservative think tanks, such as the Heritage Foundation, have erroneously propounded this idea time and again while research from a Harris survey conducted recently roundly contradicts them. Eighty-six percent of Americans participate in arts programming. Sixty-one percent are willing to be taxed five dollars or more as opposed to the current funding at forty cents per capita. Seventy-nine percent say yes to public funding for the arts, and fifty-seven percent say yes to federal arts funding."

Despite these numbers, some members of Congress are working tirelessly to restrict not only the funding of the arts but also free expression within those groups. Baldwin suggested that "one more legislative issue that will affect the arts is the effort to restrict any advocacy by nonprofit groups that receive any government funds or by any of their affiliated groups." The right of individuals or groups to talk with government officials is perhaps one of the greatest liberties protected by the First Amendment. This type of measure would clearly hold the First Amendment rights of these groups hostage — saying, in effect, if you want money, keep your mouth closed. Baldwin called these measures "nothing less than a virulent form of unconstitutional silencing of the creative not-for-profit community who must not be asked to surrender their rights in exchange for government dollars."

GRANDMA PAINTS THE TOWN

Washington, D.C., is not the only place in the country where government officials need to learn about free expression. Maxine Henderson is a grandmother in Murfreesboro, Tennessee. She is also an artist who taught the city officials there something about the First Amendment. Henderson painted a portrait of a partially nude woman. She called her painting *Gwen*. As a federal judge later described the painting, *Gwen* is a "seated female, legs crossed at the knees, with her left arm draped across her chest."[7] The painting was displayed in the Murfreesboro City Hall as part of an art show.

Assistant School Superintendent Laurie Crowder complained to city officials that she was offended by the painting, and in October 1995, she filed a sexual harassment claim. City attorney Thomas Reed argued that the painting created a hostile work environment. City officials removed the portrait and rewrote the art policy to give the manager authority to reject sexually or racially offensive works.[8] Maxine Henderson filed a lawsuit alleging that the censorship of her work violated her right to free expression under the First Amendment.

U.S. District Judge Thomas Higgins agreed with Henderson. He found that Murfreesboro had established a limited public forum when they began the art exhibit. Accordingly, Henderson had a First Amendment right to display her work in City Hall. The case took two years and cost Henderson more than $30,000, although her claim was for one dollar in damages and attorneys' fees. The judge is reviewing Henderson's legal fees to make that award, although Henderson herself is unhappy that taxpayers have to pay the bill for the misdeeds of a few officials, and she is a bit miffed at her own attorneys for generating such large fees.[9]

ART UNDER SIEGE

Maxine Henderson's case drew some attention from around the country, but Americans often never learn of many incidents of artistic censorship. People for the American Way has been tracking attacks on artistic expression through its artsave project. In 1996, the group issued its fourth report — with some startling figures. In 1995, the artsave project identified 137 incidents in which artistic expression was placed in jeopardy "because of its viewpoint, message, or content" or because the artist was denied access to a previously open venue.[10]

The report noted that 74 percent of the reported incidents were "attacks on the 'traditional' fine arts" and that 26 percent of the challenges were "attempts to restrict commercial television, movies and music, as well as photographs used for advertisements." The wide range of challenges provides a sobering view of censorship in America. As with the other areas covered in this book, attacks on artistic expression can come from the left and the right — although religious conservatives lead the pack in artistic challenges, according to the report.

The effect of these challenges, as with other areas of expression, is to create self-censorship out of frustration or fear of baseless attacks. The People for the American Way report cited one example in which the Freer Gallery, a Smithsonian-affiliated museum in Washington, D.C., pulled a film from a scheduled screening because the film told "the story of a single woman who befriends a gay male couple." The museum officials worried that the sexually explicit scenes would be "exceedingly problematic" for the audience. The quiet erosion of expressive freedom is even more problematic.

LIFE IMITATES ART

Although *The People v. Larry Flynt* did not encounter censorship like the works in the People for the American Way report, it did prompt much debate when it opened nationally in January 1997. The film, directed by Milos Forman, was critically acclaimed by some and condemned by others. The detractors objected to what they considered to be a glorification of smut peddler Larry Flynt, the feisty publisher of *Hustler* magazine — saying the film made him out to be a First Amendment hero rather than someone who made his living from pornography. Flynt is known for his flamboyance and his abrasive nature, especially when faced with authority — including judges about to sentence him on obscenity charges.

Flynt is perhaps best known, though, for his legal battles, including a Supreme Court case in which he was pitted against the leader of the

Moral Majority, the Reverend Jerry Falwell. Flynt won that case, which yielded a victory for the First Amendment by not enabling public figures to get around First Amendment defenses by filing lawsuits for emotional distress. Flynt's life, including the time he spent as a born-again Christian, was characterized in the film as a series of problems, including an assassination attempt that rendered him a paraplegic. The discussion that the film generated was a healthy debate over core First Amendment values, which also proves that films can have an impact in setting social agendas. Perhaps that is the unintended lesson of *The People v. Larry Flynt*. Americans should pause before they try to censor artistic expression, for motion pictures, books, television shows, plays, music, paintings, photographs, and other works of art can be springboards for public discourse and vehicles for learning about ourselves and the society in which we live.

SINGING THE OLD SONGS

Long before she became the nation's second lady, Tipper Gore, wife of Vice President Al Gore, led a national campaign to clean up song lyrics. Fearing that the nation's children were being exposed to violent and sexual messages through today's music, but understanding the First Amendment's prohibition against banning such expression, Mrs. Gore sought to amend these record labels with a "scarlet letter," a warning to parents that the lyrics were objectionable. To help soften any First Amendment concerns, she and others sought the *voluntary* cooperation of the music industry in affixing these warning labels. While *voluntary* is the operative word here, the not-so-subtle pressure placed on music industry executives, and trickling down to the artists themselves, led to this cooperation. The music industry recognized that holding back the tide of censorship in this manner might deflect future attempts by governmental forces to mandate such labeling. With some notable exceptions — such as the "Cop Killer" song controversy with rapper Ice-T — voluntary record labeling seemed to satisfy the appetite of the would-be censors for a few years. But as we reached the midpoint of the decade, some lawmakers, pressured by constituents in at least seven states, pushed for more control. An industry interest group, Rock Out Censorship (ROC), reported in 1995 that Washington, Pennsylvania, South Carolina, and Montana were all "thinking about making it a crime to either buy or sell — or both — music that features the music industry's so-called voluntary parental warning sticker."[11]

In fact, lawmakers in those states did more than think about it, they introduced legislation to enact such sanctions — starting in Washington State with the Erotic Music Bill, which was declared unconstitutional. A new measure came back to the state house as the Harmful Materials to Minors Bill, which would establish "adults only" sections in record stores. Pennsylvania's House Bill No. 377 placed a minimum age requirement of eighteen years on buying or selling music with the warning label. South Carolina's Senate Bill No. 127 created felonies for sellers of the stickered albums. Montana's House Bill No. 83 also created stiff criminal penalties for music retailers. Additionally, Louisiana wanted to establish a $1,000 fine or a six-month prison term for those retailers selling recordings with "lyrics harmful to minors." Similar bills were introduced in New York and New Mexico.

This snowballing threat prompted some retailers to rethink their musical inventories. Some of the nation's largest retailers, including WalMart, decided to not stock CDs with the parental advisory label.[12] Some 2,300 WalMarts now shrink-wrap CD packages and mark them as "clean," "edited," or "sanitized for your protection."[13] Obviously, business principles dictate that if the stores refuse to carry such material, it is not worth producing. That message is precisely what music censorship advocates hoped to convey to the record companies with these campaigns. Some of the same players who wish to clean up trash talk TV have gravitated to this campaign as well. U.S. Senators Joseph Lieberman (D-Connecticut) and Sam Nunn (D-Georgia, now retired) again joined forces with moralist William Bennett and activist C. Delores Tucker to combat sexual and prodrug lyrics.

They hoped to pressure the music industry to discontinue production of such songs.[14] Needless to say, if retailers capitulate, the recording artists will be forced to respond. The result will be a cleverly camouflaged attack on free expression. Proponents argue that there is no First Amendment problem. In fact, they maintain, there is no government infringement involved. Technically speaking, they are correct: No First Amendment violation exists, strictly speaking. The process works as follows: Advocates of cleaning up lyrics engage in a high-profile media blitz, and the retailers respond to the pressure by removing objectionable material. The result is that producers are forced to change music content to satisfy retailers. Nevertheless, a government nexus does exist. United States Senators are arguably enough of a government connection to take the campaign out of the purely private realm. Granted, this argument is probably not enough to win in court, but a legal victory here is not as important as the very fact that the government, through some high-profile representatives, is playing an extremely influential role in effecting a change in the content of American music. Artists who wish to make their living from the sales of their music (commercial musicians) will be forced to respond. The success these advocates have found in this "voluntary" process is encouraging further and more pronounced efforts to affect entertainment content — especially on broadcast television.

THE NEW MEANING OF TV RATINGS

Even those Americans whose only connection to the television industry is to watch TV know what is meant by the term "TV ratings." For decades the term has meant the estimated number of viewers watching a particular program during a particular time period. This may be a simplistic account of what ratings are, but it will suffice to make the point that people have a general understanding of the term. This is going to change because the public's familiarity with this definition of "TV ratings" will soon be supplanted by the new system of rating the content of television programs that has been developed by entertainment industry executives in "voluntary cooperation" with Congress — more specifically, to enable the operation of the V-chip technology that will allow parents to block out television programming they find objectionable.

The V-chip is mandated by the Telecommunications Act of 1996, signed into law on February 8, 1996, by President Bill Clinton. It requires television manufacturers to install this locking-out technology in all newly manufactured sets. Of course, the technology is useless without some way to categorize the programs on television. In similar fashion to voluntary music labeling, discussed above, the government (this time directly through Congress) called upon the television entertainment industry to cooperate by developing a self-policing rating system. At first the entertainment industry balked at the notion, calling it censorship. In a stark turnabout, however, the industry decided to go along. The result was a new ratings code. The plan calls for several ratings: TV-G (general audiences); TV-PO (parental guidance); TV-M (mature audiences); and TV-14 (not suitable for children under age fourteen). Children's shows will be rated TV-Y (suitable for all ages) and TV-Y7 (suitable for ages seven and up).

Activists, including the V-chip's main congressional sponsor, Rep. Edward Markey (D-Massachusetts), and the Children's Defense Fund, sharply criticized the proposed system because it distinguished the programs based on age rather than content (the "V" in V-chip stands for "violence"). What these advocates were hoping to accomplish was an indictment of violent programming on television. The system created by the industry does not enable them to highlight and vilify the objectionable content. Ringing endorsements of the proposed ratings system did not materialize. President Clinton adopted a wait-and-see attitude, saying instead, "It is a huge step forward over what we have now, which is nothing."[15]

Others chimed in with a similar stance. The

Washington Post's Tom Shales wrote, "Most of the trashing [of the ratings system] is going on in Washington, by naysaying members of Congress and know-it-all advocacy groups."[16] Shales said the voluntary system should be given a chance, though he recognized that Washington might be operating under a different definition of "voluntary": "The system is called 'voluntary' even though it was created under duress from Congress and the Federal Communications Commission. Congress has repeatedly threatened to impose a system of its own, which of course would be government censorship and thus eventually would be thrown out by the courts — a little inconvenience called the First Amendment would come into play."

On February 7, 1997, the Federal Communications Commission asked for comments from interested parties. On April 8, 1997, Representative Markey and twenty-one other members of Congress sent a letter expressing their concerns: "It is our view that the age-based ratings system proposed by the industry undermines the usefulness of the V-chip to such an extent that the purposes of the statute cannot be fulfilled." The letter went to express a belief that the purpose of the statute is to help parents screen out shows with violent or sexual content.

Interest groups also responded to the FCC inquiry. The Benton Foundation, a telecommunications group, echoed Markey's and his colleagues' complaint about the industry's proposal: "The Benton Foundation does not find the industry's proposal acceptable to satisfy the concerns of Congress. The industry proposes an age-based instead of a content-ratings system. The proposal attempts to decide what age group programming is appropriate for instead of informing parents what type of material (violent, sexual, etc.) is contained in an upcoming show." The Benton Foundation encouraged the FCC to allow for other ratings systems to operate side-by-side with the industry system. The Children's Television Consortium agreed, saying the industry proposal is acceptable, provided that "such an open system will enable independent, qualified rating services in addition to the industry services to distribute their rating and content code to parents and will enable parents to select a rating service of their choice."

Once again, television industry officials caved in to the pressure by the government and others and created a ratings system based on content. The new designations include S for sexual content, D for suggestive dialogue, V for violence, and FV for fantasy violence.

In the final analysis, regardless of the rating system adopted, the result will once again be indirect government control over the content of expression on television, a consequence well recognized by those in Hollywood who make television programs. Carmen Finestra, one of the creators and executive producers of the hit television series *Home Improvement*, expressed concern about the motivations behind those pushing for this influence over television program content. "I think the motivation behind it is political and not aesthetic or anything else. I honestly feel Paul Simon, [Bob] Dole, all these people are out to make a point. [Bill] Clinton, too, who said in his state-of-the-union address that something has to be done about the violence on television which permeates the media all day, every day, every hour. Now, if that's not demagoguery, I don't know what is," Finestra said. The onetime supervising producer of *The Cosby Show* recognizes that the general public is genuinely concerned about what they are seeing on television: "The population would like somebody to step forward and take some responsibility. I could say that the attack by Congress has put the fire under the feet of the network executives, who obviously are in a business where the perception of the public is important to them."

CURTAILING CREATIVITY

Advocates of the V-chip and the ratings system designed to go hand in hand with it are now comfortable in their belief that the First Amendment is not affected at all by the process they have endorsed. But free expression is hurt, and the ultimate loser will be the general viewing public. Creators of television programming are keenly aware of the effect the ratings will have on their ability to produce the shows the public has come to enjoy. It is dishonest for proponents of the ratings system to characterize the system as solely a means of placing programming into convenient categories. In effect, the ratings system will send a message to producers to develop certain kinds of programming.

Once the ratings system has been in place for some time, patterns will begin to emerge. In other words, the traditional ratings system — the one that charts viewership trends — will undoubtedly produce data identifying certain demographic populations who frequently view programming in a particular category (e.g., TV-PG). Conversely, surveys will also indicate which categories are excluded the most by viewers through the V-chip. Because advertisers look for exposure to particular demographics and typically avoid controversy, they will select and avoid shows based on the categories into which they fall.

Consequently, advertising decisions will be based not only on a particular show but also on entire categories of shows. This message will be heard in Hollywood, and producers will have to adjust creative elements accordingly.

According to Finestra, the process was flawed from the outset.

My concern with the government is the whole ratings system. I feel the people who were invited to the White House some months ago to have this conference on having a ratings system all represented studio heads and network executives. There really were no creative people there. There were no producers. There was no one there to represent the voice of the creator to say "Let's come up with a system that is objective and fair."

Finestra fears the political ratings system will become the subject of "the furthest forces to the right." The result would be the suppression of positive messages as well as those intended to be avoided. The definitions of violence and sexual content might be so far-reaching, according to Finestra, as to include positive messages such as "teenage responsibility or any discussion of sex, even if it is abstinence." Finestra also said he cannot get past the political motivations involved and the resulting irony. "I'm also concerned about people like Bob Dole who say that a Schwarzenegger movie is okay — that's family entertainment — when I think that's the worst kind of violence because it's cartoonish. People just sit in the theaters and cheer while somebody's head flies across the room."

Finestra and others believe the ratings system, in its application, will be fundamentally unfair and will probably fall apart. Network executives agreed to cooperate because the attacks on television content became vicious and they wanted to be seen as responsible citizens. But the esprit de corps will likely wane as revenues decline. Finestra thinks one result of the ratings system will be that more viewers will flock to cable channels. "Right now cable has filled the need even for those who can't get shows for their children. Nickelodeon is one of the most popular channels for young kids. It has such identifiability that kids just come home and turn it on. The same will be true for sexual content and violence." Cable stands ready to meet that demand.

The bottom line for program creators will be the pressure put on them by network executives to make television shows that will pass muster. As Finestra put it, "If I don't like it, I can go off and start my own theater group, but let's be honest . . . everybody who is in television is making a lot of money and they understand completely that they are making programs that are sponsored. If the studios for whom they work, which now are these giant corporations [don't want a particular show], they will be told no, and what will they do? Quit their multimillion-dollar development deals? No. They'll go right along with it."

Those in front of the camera recognize the sensitive nature of this discussion and the public's frustration with television content. Actor Alec Baldwin said he sympathizes with parents who do not want their kids exposed to some of the material on television. Baldwin started his acting career on television but soon thereafter turned to motion pictures, where he makes most of his living now. He said:

> The corporate end of the business has come under tremendous fire from people about what is available on television, and quite frankly, I understand those people who are concerned about television content. Presumably exhibitors of motion pictures are required to follow the motion picture code and not admit people to motion pictures who don't belong there, who are not the right age. Television is a completely different ball game so the debate about television is something that I am far more sensitive to. I think censorship in movies is ridiculous, but as far as television is concerned, the sex and violence that parents want to protect their children from seeing on broadcast television, I am a little more sensitive to and a little more understanding of that, although I don't think the ratings system is the answer.

If the television industry had not responded with a ratings system, the government would have had to find some alternative because the congressionally mandated V-chip cannot work without one. In terms of free expression, then, the ratings system will influence the content of messages on television, and the only reason it is not a First Amendment infringement is that the industry itself developed it. The effect on the content of expression, though, is the same, but the government has come up with a convenient tactic to remove itself from constitutional prohibitions. This coercive camouflage is the same type used in the other areas of expression highlighted throughout this book. The new wave of suppression simply requires the removal of the First Amendment barrier, and it's becoming increasingly popular.

The arts and entertainment industry is a popular battle target for opponents of free expression. First, the area is ripe for controversy, for if the work at issue crosses the border from artistic expression into obscenity, it loses First Amendment protection. Second, in the popular debate over family values, cleaning up television is the "poster child." Advocates for sanitized television can easily exploit the harm-for-children argument. Finally, many Americans, stretched to the limit in terms of their own personal finances, are not likely to object strongly if federal funding for the arts was to disappear.

9

Money Talks — But Is It

Protected Speech?

"In the free society ordained by our Constitution it is not the government, but the people — individually as citizens and candidates and collectively as associations and political committees — who must retain control over the quantity and range of debate on public issues in a political campaign."

— *Buckley v. Valeo*, 1976

If citizens were told that they have a right to travel but that they could spend only $100 doing so, they would not really have a right to travel. That analogy was used by Senator Mitch McConnell (R-Kentucky) to explain how campaign finance reform rubs up against the First Amendment right of free speech. McConnell was addressing a group of journalists and others at a National Press Club luncheon in Washington, D.C., on March 19, 1997 — one day after the Senate voted down (by a 61-to-38 margin) a constitutional amendment that would have, in McConnell's words, "blow[n] a big hole in the First Amendment."

The proposed amendment would have bound candidates for federal office to government-ordained spending and contribution limits. The measure, which would have needed a two-thirds majority to move on to the states for ratification, would be necessary to set such limits because the United States Supreme Court ruled in 1976 that expenditure limits were unconstitutional, saying essentially that money is tantamount to speech in the political arena. McConnell said the thirty-eight senators who voted for the amendment were engaged in "an all-out assault on the First Amendment in the name of reform." He sharply criticized the senators for trying to "roll back two centuries of political freedom."

McConnell is a Republican leader, and for more than two decades he has opposed campaign finance reform measures that would scuttle First Amendment protections — even when those measures were introduced by members of his own party (Republican Senator Arlen Specter of Pennsylvania was a co-sponsor of this last proposed constitutional amendment). McConnell has adhered to his view that politicians have a right to communicate views to their constituents in an unfettered manner, and says that "virtually every means of distributing ideas require the expenditure of money."

McConnell's stance is not popular. The public generally supports campaign finance reform. In fact, a recent *New York Times*/CBS News poll on the country's campaign finance system revealed that nine out of ten Americans believe fundamental changes are needed. But that same group holds little hope of seeing such reform enacted by the very politicians who benefit from campaign contributions and expenditures. *Reform* is one of those political buzzwords that resonate well with most of America, but limiting speech, even when couched in terms of limiting spending, would take some of the wind out of the First Amendment. Part of the image problem the First Amendment faces in this particular political battle is that cries for reform typically are heard in times of scandal, when the public is fed up with politics in general. This latest go-around was no exception. Both Democrats and Republicans had been embroiled in campaign finance scandals, including contributions from foreign businesses, when the seeds of reform germinated in the politically muddy field.

NO STRANGER TO SCANDAL

After the Watergate scandal took center stage in 1972, politicians needed to do something to clean up their collective act. Recognizing that some of the money raised for that year's presidential campaign had been expended in furtherance of criminal activity, Congress decided that some finance reform was in order. The result was an amendment to the 1971 Federal Election Campaign Act. The amendment restricted political contributions to federal candidates to $1,000 from an individual or group and $5,000 from a political action committee (PAC) per election (with a $25,000 annual limitation overall). Moreover, the amendment limited the amount of money that candidates and their committees could spend during the election.

This prix fixe means of operation would have obvious consequences on campaigns. Limiting both contributions and expenditures would mean that candidates and their handlers would need to make even more strategic decisions on where to place advertisements, where to give speeches, and how to get the most overall exposure for the least amount of money. Clearly, some audiences would be missed. But if the transmission of political messages were impinged by this regulation, First Amendment considerations would clearly come into play.

SUPREME INTERVENTION

Throughout this book, the First Amendment has played a central role in a diverse group of subjects. In most of those instances, its role is apparent. Many Americans, however, have great difficulty grasping how the First Amendment figures into the mix of campaign financing. The Supreme Court explained the relationship in a lengthy, unsigned, opinion in *Buckley v. Valeo* in 1976.[1] But some experts, who understand the Court's position, simply do not agree with it.

The Supreme Court heard the challenge to campaign finance reform on November 10, 1975. The Court had heard many political speech cases in its history. In fact, it was pretty well settled law that political speech deserves the highest form of protection from government infringement.[2] Some legal scholars had long argued for absolute First Amendment protection of political speech because discussion of candidates, their views, and their qualifications should be strongly encouraged. A democracy best functions when the electorate takes an active role and casts informed votes. So the Court was presented a fundamental dilemma: "[W]hether the specific legislation that Congress has enacted interfere[d] with First Amendment freedoms. . . ."

One side of the case argued that any effect on speech was incidental and that the legislation was aimed at conduct (contributions and expenditures), not speech. The opposing argument was that this particular conduct goes to the very heart of political discourse and thus directly impinges on speech. The Court refused to accept the view that this legislation merely regulated conduct. In its per curiam opinion, the Court wrote: "A restriction on the amount of money a person or group can spend on political communication during a campaign necessarily reduces the quantity of expression by restricting the number of issues discussed, the depth of their exploration, and the size of the audience reached."[3] In a footnote, the justices made a useful analogy: "Being free to engage in unlimited political expression subject to a ceiling on expenditures is like being free to drive an automobile as far and as often as one desires on a single tank of gasoline."

Proponents of campaign finance reform had suggested to the Court that such measures really only amounted to time, place, and manner restrictions on speech, something the Court many times had ruled would be permissible if they furthered an important government interest — and provided that an alternative means of getting one's message across was available. An illustration of a time-place-manner restriction is an ordinance prohibiting the distribution of literature on the boarding ramps at an airport. Notice that such a regulation does not address the content of the message. It merely regulates the time, place, and manner of delivery. Traditionally, these restrictions have had an easier time passing constitutional muster.

In the campaign finance situation, however, the Court did not see the restrictions in that fashion. "The critical difference between this case and those time, place, and manner cases is that the present Act's contribution and expenditure limitations impose direct quantity restrictions on political communication and association by persons, groups, candidates, and political parties in addition to any reasonable time, place, and manner regulations otherwise imposed."[4] The Court viewed these restrictions in pragmatic terms. The justices recognized that money is equal to speech, and that maxim was not simply a theoretical construct in political discourse but instead had a very real impact on the "quantity and diversity of political speech."[5] The Court also looked at the changing nature of political campaigns and the expense associated with communicating a message: "The distribution of the humblest handbill or leaflet entails printing, paper, and circulation costs. Speeches and rallies generally necessitate hiring a hall and publicizing the event. The electorate's increasing dependence on television, radio, and other mass media for news and information has made these expensive modes of communication indispensable instruments of effective political speech."[6] The Court reasoned that limiting this expression, although couched in neutral terms in the act, in essence was a restriction on political expression, which has long been recognized as "at the core of our electoral process and of the First Amendment freedoms."[7]

The Court was less troubled by the act's limitations on contributions, although it recognized that some First Amendment implications exist with respect to those limitations as well. In contrast to the expenditure limitation, though, the Court found that "a limitation upon the amount that any person or group may contribute to a candidate or political committee entails only a marginal restriction upon a contributor's ability to engage in free communication."[8] The Court rationalized these limitations by finding contributions to be more of a symbolic form of communication: "A contribution serves as a general expression of support for a candidate and his views, but does not communicate the underlying basis for the support. The quantity of communication by the contributor does not increase perceptibly with the size of his contribution, since the expression rests solely on the undifferentiated, symbolic act of contributing."[9] Accordingly, the Court upheld the $1,000 contribution limitation under the act, finding little impact on the First Amendment because the "limitations in themselves do not undermine to any material degree the potential for robust and effective discussion of candidates and campaign issues by individual citizens, associations, the institutional press, candidates, and political parties."[10] Moreover, any incidental impact on speech would be justified by balancing it against the greater public good of ending big-money contributions to candidates and thus reducing the opportunity for corruption.

BUCKLEY'S REVENGE

Against this background, reformers today must work around this notion, now firmly embedded into the law, that money is speech in the political arena. In the more than two decades since *Buckley* was decided, the sums of money necessary to mount an effective campaign for federal office have skyrocketed. Candidates for congressional seats spend millions of dollars to be elected to a seat they might hold for only two years. The practical effect is that congressional candidates are essentially always campaigning for office, and thus are always raising and spending money.

The constant jockeying for campaign contributions from more and varied sources also raises questions about the payback for those contributions. In a system where money is the major way of getting across a message, the question becomes: How beholden are members of Congress or senators to the sources of their campaign contributions? In Washington, the flip side of this issue, which also raises some First Amendment questions, is that contributions are not just given to support an ideology of a particular candidate, they are given to curry favor and provide access to a particular lawmaker. Some reformers thus look to cut out access — in the form of lobbying restrictions — but that, too, has raised

First Amendment questions, not only about free speech considerations but also about the right of the people to petition the government for a redress of grievances.

RALLYING TO AMEND THE CONSTITUTION

Campaign finance reform is a favorite topic among Americans. Few people do not have an opinion on the current system, and most favor some kind of reform. Most Americans also believe that the current system of financing election campaigns favors the two major political parties in this country. But because attempts at reform are mostly these two parties working to ensure that neither one gets the edge over the other, any hopes for real reform are usually dashed in the process of partisan politics. The First Amendment is the easy target. After all, the Supreme Court has ruled that it is the Constitution that makes it impossible to enact spending caps on politicians. Thus, politicians who adopt the publicly popular stance of "Let's clean up campaign financing" know that they are limited in what can be realistically accomplished — and that the First Amendment provides an easy scapegoat when attempts at reform are unsuccessful. In the end, the issue is a good public relations tool for them. Once again, the First Amendment suffers the image blow.

Instead of looking for creative ways to accomplish true reform, the focus is on what supporters of finance reform call the Supreme Court's flawed opinion in *Buckley*. When Gene Karpinski, executive director of the United States Public Interest Research Group, testified about campaign finance reform on February 27, 1997, before the House Subcommittee on the Constitution, he took the opportunity to slam the *Buckley* ruling.

Even if First Amendment considerations applied (and we believe they don't), we regard the narrow test to be insufficient. Other constitutional considerations — of equal protection of the law, of the integrity of the election process, and of the preservation of a democratic form of government — have been entirely ignored by these Court rulings. We believe the current system of campaign financing does far more violence to the Constitution in these regards than would spending and contribution limits supported by a majority of the body politic, and equally and fairly applied to all citizens and candidates.

Senator Tom Daschle, in a March 12, 1997, press release announcing the upcoming vote on Senate Joint Resolution 18 (the proposed constitutional amendment), set forth the issue.

Advocates of the amendment conclude that there are two possible approaches to the problems associated with the *Buckley* decision. The first is legislating around *Buckley* by making limits voluntary. Proponents believe that this will probably not work. They doubt that such legislation could be enacted and believe that it probably would not hold up under strict scrutiny analysis which would be applied by federal courts. Furthermore, voluntary limits are unenforceable. Wealthy candidates or candidates with a heavy fundraising advantage have no incentive to limit their expenditures voluntarily. The second solution is a constitutional amendment, essentially overturning the *Buckley* decision with regard to mandatory spending limits.

The day before Daschle's news release, Senator Arlen Specter and Senator Ernest Hollings (D-South Carolina) held a briefing on their proposed constitutional amendment. Specter used the example of his own campaign in a 1976 primary against the late Senator John Heinz.

In my judgment, that opinion [*Buckley*] of the Supreme Court was not well-founded, because there is nothing about spending money in an election campaign which involves speech for certain people and not for others. That particular decision was especially meaningful for me because I was in the middle of a primary election campaign with my good friend, John Heinz, and we later became very, very close working senators on the Senate floor. The law provided that from a state the size of Pennsylvania, someone was limited to spend $35,000, which was about as much money as I had. In the middle of our campaign for the Senate primary on January 30th of 1976, the Supreme Court of the United States said any individual could spend millions, and John did. But my brother, who could have helped me finance my campaign, was limited to $1,000. So Morton Specter's speech was limited to $1,000 but Senator Heinz's was unlimited.

The U.S. Public Interest Research Group's Gene Karpinski has argued that amending the Constitution is the way to proceed. "Our democracy is in grave danger because of big money in politics. The public is clamoring for reform. The antidemocratic *Buckley* decision stands in the way of this. It is time to overturn *Buckley*, and a constitutional amendment is necessary to do so."

Other critics of the *Buckley* decision include the Brennan Center for Justice at New York University, named for retired Supreme Court Justice William J. Brennan. The center's stance is somewhat ironic given the fact that although the Court's opinion in *Buckley* was unsigned, Brennan is widely suspected to have been a principal author. E. Joshua Rosenkranz, a former Brennan law clerk who now heads the center, said Brennan made the founders of the center promise not to be the "Brennan Defense Fund."[11] Another strange bedfellow in the fight to overturn *Buckley* is New York University law professor Burt Neuborne, who once served as the ACLU's legal director and defended the decision on First Amendment grounds.[12]

Also appearing before the House Subcommittee on the Constitution was Lloyd N. Cutler, a prominent Washington attorney who argued a portion of the *Buckley* case. He told members of the House subcommittee that a constitutional amendment was not necessary to accomplish what should be the goals of the reformers:

> The only need for constitutional amendment is to reverse *Buckley* as to regulation of independent expenditures on behalf of candidates and candidate expenditures from personal and family funds. But in my view these issues are not at the heart of the problem. The heart of the problem is twofold: (a) capping the amount of soft money used by party and election committees for the benefit of or coordinated with specific candidates, and (b) capping contributions to PACs and expenditures by PACs on behalf of or coordinated with candidates.

Cutler also explained that no amendment may

be needed under *Buckley*. "What is needed is congressional willingness to enact the necessary legislation," he testified.

To effect campaign finance reform, the politicians and the public they serve need to move beyond finger-pointing toward the Supreme Court and a convenient assault on the First Amendment. Common Cause, a congressional watchdog group that favors campaign finance reform, has called attempts to amend the Constitution a diversion from more realistic measures that essentially gives Congress an escape from hard-core finance reform.[13]

THE MCCAIN-FEINGOLD BILL

One of the main pieces of finance reform legislation to hit Capitol Hill in the 105th session of Congress is S. 25 — the Bipartisan Campaign Reform Act of 1997, commonly classified by the surnames of its primary sponsors, Senator John McCain (R-Arizona) and Senator Russ Feingold (D-Wisconsin). A companion bill — H.R. 493 — was introduced in the House of Representatives on the same day, January 21, 1997. Senator McCain told his colleagues in the Senate that "passage of campaign finance reform is necessary if we are to curb the public's growing cynicism for politics and Congress in particular." McCain said he harbored no illusion that passage of this bill would come easily, but he pledged a spirit of cooperation to senators on both sides of the aisle as he underscored the critical need for reform: "Twenty-five years after Watergate, the electoral system is out of control. Our elections are awash in money which is flowing into the system at record levels. Some public interest groups estimate that when all is said and done, that nearly $1 billion will have been spent during this last election cycle. Something must be done."

As is typical in Washington, once a bill is introduced, it is marked up for committee and the Sunday morning talk shows begin deliberations on it. This topic, with its First Amendment as well as hot political implications, was ripe fodder for talk shows. After the constitutional amendment was defeated, NBC's *Meet the Press* took up the topic of the McCain-Feingold Bill with former vice president Walter Mondale and former senators Howard Baker and Nancy Kassebaum Baker. *Washington Post* reporter and columnist David Broder asked Mondale if he was aware that the ACLU had found the bill (which Mondale supported) to be "fatally and fundamentally flawed when measured against the First Amendment?" Underlying Broder's question was the notion of spending limitations as tantamount to restricting speech. Mondale noted that he disagreed with the ACLU's analysis of the legislation: "What this bill does is seek to put in place incentives that would encourage people running for federal office to accept ceilings and other restraints on how they campaign."[14]

Nancy Kassebaum Baker acknowledged some problems with the legislation, but said some rough spots are bound to occur in any legislation of this magnitude, especially since nothing like this had occurred since the original laws were passed back in the mid-1970s.

Common Cause has backed the McCain-Feingold Bill as providing the framework for effective campaign finance reform and has embarked on a petition drive to muster support in what it is calling a "Declaration for Independence." Other groups are not as sure about congressional attempts to police itself. The National Right to Life Committee (NRLC) attacked the legislation, saying it contained "multiple, unprecedented mechanisms to ration and suppress communications to the public regarding policy issues and the positions of those who hold and seek public office on those issues." NRLC was referring to provisions in the bill restricting issue advocacy (in which a candidate's name or likeness appears in ads paid for by advocacy groups).

PRIVATE SECTOR EFFORTS

Other grassroots groups have proposed different ways to accomplish a reformed campaign financing system. Public Campaign, a nonpartisan group interested in "taking special-interest money out of America's elections," has called for "Clean Money Campaign Reform." According to information on the group's web site,[15] its solution is to provide candidates with "a set amount of public financing for their election campaigns if they reject private money, limit their spending, and shorten their campaigns." One of the selling points the group puts forth is that this proposal will pass constitutional muster because it is not out of step with the Supreme Court's decisions in this area.

The one central theme that appears to be part of most realistic reformers is that whatever limits are placed on spending must be voluntary. In other words, except for those who would like to amend the Constitution, most proponents of campaign finance reform recognize the weighty First Amendment considerations involved in this process. Although they might not like the notion of money as speech, they at least appreciate this factor and now may perhaps move beyond the stalemate that ordinarily blocks movement on this topic.

The Brookings Institution has spent considerable time and resources examining campaign financing. The Washington-based think tank has stated in a position paper that the nation's campaign financing system is in a crisis state: "We need an approach that breaks us out of the unproductive framework — Democrats insisting on a bottom line of tough spending limits and public financing, Republicans insisting on a bottom line of no spending limits and no public financing — that has doomed any constructive change for decades."[16] The position paper recognizes that a constitutional amendment is not likely in the current political climate and urges reformers to take into consideration the First Amendment requirements set forth by the Supreme Court in *Buckley v. Valeo*. Brookings's suggested approach looks at five areas for change: (1) regulating "soft money," funds that fall outside of current federal regulation, to "create one pot of national party money that has similar fund-raising qualifications to the money raised for candidates, namely, no corporate and union funds and limits on sums from individuals"; (2) treating issue advocacy advertisements as campaign ads (subject to rules on independent expenditures) if they use a federal candidate's name or likeness within ninety days of an election or primary; (3) creation of a "broadcast bank" with vouchers for federal candidates to purchase time for political spots on radio and television; (4) use of incentives to encourage small individual contributions to candidates, and conversely disincentives for large contributtons; and (5) changes in the structure of the Federal Elections Commission (FEC) to aid enforcement of campaign laws.[17]

Politicians, advocacy groups, and individuals from all corners of the country have weighed in on the campaign financing system. Most would welcome reform. They just differ on what the reform should be and how to accomplish it. In that respect, this dilemma is no different from any other First Amendment problem. On May 12, 1997, the Federal Elections Commission released a report — in effect, a report card on itself — marking the twentieth anniversary of its creation. The opening pages of the report set forth the reasons Congress passed the legislation creating the commission in the first place. The report stated:

> The regulation of federal campaigns emanated from a congressional judgment that our representative form of government needed protection from the corrosive influence of unlimited and undisclosed political contributions. The laws were designed to ensure that candidates in federal elections were not — or did not appear to be — beholden to a narrow group of people. Taken together, it was hoped the laws would sustain and promote citizen confidence and participation in the democratic process.

In short, not much has changed in the commission's twenty-year history. The legislative intent in the Federal Election Campaign Act, passed more than two decades ago, is essentially the same as the intentions of the lawmakers in the current round of legislation — cleaning up the system and restoring the confidence of the electorate.

A notation in the FEC report should give Americans something to think about as well. It notes that the historical origins of campaign financing date back to 1791 (incidentally, the same year the First Amendment was ratified), when supporters and opponents of Alexander Hamilton both published newspapers designed to influence voters. In the 1800s, campaign expenditures grew along with the voting population. According to the report, corruption was minimal during the pre-Civil War period but became rampant during the postwar days.

In the end, the system of campaign financing is going to be whatever lawmakers make it. In other words, a willingness to agree to what the rules are and then to live by them is crucial to any real reform. In the public battle over reform, the First Amendment is a convenient red herring, but real reform can be accomplished despite the *Buckley* case if politicians wish to work for real reform. By throwing their hands up in the air and blaming the Supreme Court for the mess campaign financing is in, lawmakers may be engaging in good political theater, but in reality they are merely sidestepping the task of reform.

10

Freedom's Future

"The First Amendment presupposes that right conclusions are more likely to be gathered out of a multitude of tongues than through any kind of authoritative selection. To many this is, and always will be, folly. But we have staked upon it our all."

— Judge Learned Hand, c. 1950

For centuries sages have claimed an ability to predict the future. From clairvoyants to fortune-tellers, from weather forecasters to political pundits, some people have made a living from trying to satisfy our curiosity about what is going to happen next. But predicting the future is never certain. Curiously, the law has developed in such a way that predicting the future is theoretically made easier. Our system of jurisprudence is based on the concept of stare decisis — "let the decision stand." That Latin phrase has come to signify the legal system's reliance on and adherence to precedent. In other words, when courts are faced with making a decision, they look to past decisions in fashioning their responses to similar situations.

Without a respect for precedent, the law would be chaos. Still, just as weather forecasters sometimes miss the call, so, too, do courts — and sometimes it is by design. The law evolves over time, and courts deliberately change things. In the late 1800s, segregation was blessed by a Supreme Court opinion.[1] In 1954, the Supreme Court reversed that position in *Brown v. Board of Education.*[2] The fluidity of the law is obviously a positive attribute, for it permits subtle, if not radical, changes when necessary to correct injustices. Nonetheless, a strong base, the Constitution, provides the steady framework for a functioning society.

So it is not entirely folly to spend a chapter here looking to the future of the First Amendment and trying to engage in a bit of forecasting. With more than two hundred years of history, some of it stormy, some of it calm, we have a considerable basis on which to rely. Technology may muddy the road, but the greater threat to the First Amendment may be the growing restlessness the public seems to have with unfettered expression.

Throughout the past nine chapters, various infringements, remedies, and outrages have been presented, all in an effort to convince the readers of this book of a fundamental concept: Free speech is needed in a democracy. People must have the ability to communicate with government whenever they wish. They cannot fear reprisal for participating in this bold experiment of government. Democratic forms of government, by definition, make provisions for public input. We rail against tyrannical forms of government under which individuals are beaten, tortured, murdered, or imprisoned for speaking out. Yet, little outrage is voiced when families in a small community in Maryland are figuratively clubbed into submission by an onerous lawsuit designed to retaliate against them and to keep them from voicing concerns to their government. Obviously, the human rights violations that come with physical violence are far worse than the quiet summons of a civil lawsuit, but the motivation and the impact on speech are the same. And Americans do not typically appear too concerned about the similarities.

Thankfully, for the most part, the United States is more genteel and respectful of the human rights of its citizens. Despite occasional incidents to the contrary (such as the shootings at Kent State in the 1970s, the MOVE bombing in Philadelphia in the 1980s, and the burning of the Branch Davidian complex in the 1990s), the government is generally not prone to violent acts, especially to quell expression. That civility lulls us all into a sense of being on automatic pilot with respect to our rights. We do not spend much time thinking about our liberties. Sure, there are some who leap into the forefront every so often to remind us. Typically, the culprit is a porno peddler, a journalist who made up quotes, an artist with a collection of homoerotic photographs, or another similar character. If James Madison were trying to garner support for his draft of the First Amendment, he probably would not have chosen these types as his spokespersons. Perhaps that is why Americans have not embraced the First Amendment as an important cause in more recent times.

Free expression cases are not the only ones in which people have had difficulty moving beyond the facts to look at the underlying policy considerations. When a suspect is arrested and is questioned by police interrogators, if that suspect is not properly informed of his rights, the information gleaned during that questioning is often inadmissible in court. Sometimes that includes a confession to a crime. The public has great trouble grasping the reason for this procedural device. After all, if someone confesses to a crime, that is perhaps the best evidence against him or her. Why should courts ever exclude such a statement? The reason is that the United States is governed by a constitution — a contract, of sorts, between the government and its people, or actually vice versa — that gives all of us certain powers and rights. The police cannot willfully violate those rights. As with other First Amendment cases, the subjects in these cases are often individuals who have committed heinous crimes and toward whom we feel we owe no particular debt. But in safeguarding the rights of these unsavory characters we protect ourselves from unwarranted intrusions by authorities. No one wants to live in a police state, and the rights embodied in the Constitution guarantee against it.

Likewise, no one wants to live in a society where we cannot speak our minds, read an uncensored newspaper, or voice our concerns to government. To ensure that does not happen, we must be willing, if not eager, to protect the rights of the underbelly of the citizenry. Too often, individuals and collectives try to distance themselves from the person or persons asserting First Amendment rights, and this can have adverse consequences — maybe not immediately, but clearly over time. As Larry Flynt, publisher of *Hustler* magazine, put it, "If the First Amendment will protect a scumbag like me, then it will protect all of you. Because I'm the worst."[3]

Lyle Denniston is one reporter who has been able to see long-term effects. He has covered the United States Supreme Court for more than three decades and is widely considered to be the dean of Supreme Court correspondents. From his vantage point inside the press office at the Supreme Court, Denniston has observed and written about constitutional law for his primary publication, the *Baltimore Sun*, along with journals and trade publications. He contends, "An illusion has been propagated that the First

Amendment is a strong barrier to suppression of speech, thought, expression generally." He has found it to be an "illusion" because "legal inhibitions upon expression are fairly easy to adopt politically." He cited the continued regulation of radio and television as an example.

The problem as Denniston sees it has much to do with perception. People become immune to government restriction. "Broadcast is a good case study because it illustrates how a perception of expression as being regulable gets started and then doesn't get questioned anymore," he said. Once such regulation is in place, people come to accept it. Denniston's point underscores the notion that over time rights begin to fade unless someone does something proactively to stop the erosion. According to the veteran Court watcher, "There is a culture in politics and in law that is unusually and perhaps spectacularly inventive in continuing to maintain a regime of control, of channeling regulation, inhibition on expression."

As this unquestioned regulation becomes more commonplace, its reach can be more globally applied. In fact, the concept of stare decisis practically ensures that this will happen. Lyle Denniston worries about this in his own profession. "One of my most deeply felt anxieties as a free citizen and as a journalist is that as the news industry becomes increasingly electrified — addicted to, dependent upon electronics — the regime of law that has been developed for the electronic press will be engrafted on the print press," he said.

As we continue to move forward in the electronic age, we may need to remind ourselves and those who make and interpret law of some fundamental notions of free speech. In essence, society may have to look at the importance of free speech throughout history, and history does indeed provide testament to the value of the First Amendment. This effort may have to spring from the grassroots level because the country's leadership has not moved in that direction. As Lyle Denniston observed, "I cannot remember when someone in a position of power and influence last stood up and said, 'We really ought to be thinking more fundamentally about this — what is the nature of expression?' "

GET OFF THE BANDWAGON
(OR SOAPBOX)

Picking on freedom of expression has become an easy sport of late, and ironically, many of the participants have taken an oath to defend the Constitution that protects free speech. It is now all too common to hear members of Congress speaking out against free speech, maybe not in so many words, but in cleverly disguised good deeds to protect society. Ironically, some of these members who would vehemently oppose a ban on assault weapons heartily endorse bully-ing Hollywood to stop portraying them in mo-tion pictures. In similar fashion, lawmakers who have done little to clean up the grotesque under-belly of American society do not want to see remnants of it on television talk shows. The mes-senger is clearly bearing the brunt of the criti-cism.

Politicians are not alone (or else they would not be politicians for long). The American public has tragically lost perspective on this issue as well. They are disgusted by what they see and hear, but instead of attacking the problem, they would rather ensure that they do not see or hear about the problem anymore. This "ostrich" approach to citizenship is further exacerbated by an "off-with-their-heads" mentality toward the communications industry. The media are not entirely blameless here, either. The forays into tabloid reporting, practiced on occasion by even legitimate news organizations, further enhance the argument that restrictions are sometimes necessary. The media could and should do a better job of polishing its own image from time to time and avoid tabloid presentation in their coverage.

The media's self-interest is at stake here as well. Juries are willing — and, in some cases, eager — to take a swing at news organizations, and they are using the club of enormous money verdicts to do the job. Typically after receiving a drumming, news executives are quick to say that news coverage will not be affected. In other words, that particular media outlet will not compromise when it comes to hard-hitting investigative reporting. This bravado hurts rather than helps the industry. First, it is not entirely truthful. Any news organization hit by a megaverdict will be affected in some way — for example, a particular story might not be pursued or at least not be pursued as vigorously. Other news organizations are also going to take a lesson from their brethren's misfortune. Second, the public needs to know that megaverdicts do harm the news organization's ability to do its job.

Viewers should be told that news outlets are less likely to use hidden cameras after the Food Lion case, and this translates into fewer stories about day-care workers slapping infants, nursing home employees refusing to feed elderly patients or change soiled bedclothes, crooked mechanics puncturing hoses when they are supposed to be repairing the car, health care workers not using proper procedures when handling body fluids, and airport baggage handlers riffling through passenger luggage. Instead of simply stating "We stand by our story and we're unfazed by the verdict," the news industry as a collective should stand up and say the American public will get less of the kind of information it needs to know because some jury thought it was important to slam the media. In short, journalism will have less of an impact. The media have to lose the arrogant posturing and show the public that they work in its best interest.

The media cannot accomplish this image job, though, by backing off a fight for First Amendment rights, particularly when the reason for doing so is the bottom line. First Amendment litigation is often a battle on principle. Ordinary citizens cannot afford to wage battles for just causes, and the media have an obligation to do it for them. When the media win such a battle, consumers of media win, too. The V-chip debacle is a good example of the media's capitulating when they should have held firm. The goodwill between broadcasters and the congressional proponents of the V-chip will undoubtedly continue to erode before the final rating system is put in place. Once broadcasters get a feel for what they are giving up (and the potential for diminishing profits), we are likely to see a major overhaul of the ratings system and probably some further encroachment on the content of broadcast television.

MEDIA MELTING POT OF GOLD

It first looked like a bright spot on the First Amendment horizon when the Libel Defense Resource Center (LDRC) reported that libel verdicts leveled off in the mid-1990s, but that good news was tempered by the astronomical judgments in both the early part of the decade and the later part of the decade. In other words, a decline in large judgments occurred for a short time, but the leveling off had to be measured against enormous verdicts in the first instance. Moreover, any decline will be tempered by the 1996 verdicts of $10 million in a case brought against ABC by a Florida banker, of more than $5 million in a case brought by a Texas state representative against a Houston television station, and the astronomical $222.7 million verdict against the *Wall Street Journal*. Despite reductions of those verdicts in some cases, the chill is still alive. Media organizations and the lawyers advising them know too well the sting of protracted litigation. Emblazoned on their minds are the megaverdicts that hit like a tornado in Philadelphia and Dallas and now in Miami and Houston. The LDRC always cautions users of its study that it is difficult to draw conclusions from the tallies of lawsuits from year to year. In other words, a good year this year is not necessarily a predictor of next year's First Amendment health.

People are certainly willing to sue and even to use litigation for something other than its intended use. Strategic Lawsuits Against Public Participation (SLAPPs) will no doubt increase as we move into the next millennium. States have been slow to enact measures to protect their citizens from such harassing measures, and the business lobby is powerful in every state. Some government officials quietly support the tactic because they tire of activists who prolong meetings or block measures with their repetitive complaints. The point that gets lost is that most people who are targets of SLAPPs are not organized protesters or activists. They are ordinary citizens who may for the first time in their lives stand up because the interest at stake is their own. The founders of this nation wanted to specifically enable this type of activity. Accordingly, they included the petition clause in the First Amendment.

EDUCATIONAL ENDEAVORS

Colleges and universities are facing major transitions into the next century. Educational costs are rising, thus diminishing the ability of some to pursue higher education. Also, the use of affirmative action principles in the admissions process has been placed in jeopardy.[4] What effect these changes will have on other preferential programs on campus remains to be seen. These changes will undoubtedly shape the debate on campuses all across the country, and some previously verboten topics (under the cloud of speech codes) will emerge. Thus, educational institutions will need to come to grips with free speech principles as well. Courts have demonstrated that they will not tolerate censorship, even in the name of creating a nonhostile environment for underrepresented groups. Those who make their living in academe must also recognize that circumventing the First Amendment is not the solution to the problem. As Dinesh D'Souza observed, "When the speech code is shut down, the professorial cabal assembles and says, listen, how can we rewrite the code or enforce it in a way that's going to keep the court off our backs and nonetheless achieve our own objectives."

This unhealthy attitude toward free speech principles that portrays the First Amendment as an obstacle is detrimental to the educational mission. Higher education must return discourse in all its forms to the forefront of the academic setting. Students and faculty must feel comfortable speaking out about issues. Currently, administrators engage in "selective prosecution," lashing out at those whose speech they disfavor — like Eden Jacobowitz's shouting "water buffalo" at the University of Pennsylvania. But those who seek to stifle such expression by burning campus newspapers, for example, feel immune from serious retribution.

Society's tolerance for this environment on college and university campuses is rapidly dissipating. Some administrators are beginning to turn up the heat on each other for fear of the public's backlash. During Penn State's 1996 commencement, the valedictorian from the business college was removed as a graduation speaker because in his speech he thanked God for his achievements. A committee comprised of faculty and staff from the business college wanted him to take out his reference to God, but the student refused. When word of this decision leaked out, it quickly spread around the country, and the public outrage was apparent. University President Graham B. Spanier quickly and publicly chastised the college's selection committee and ratified the university's commitment to free speech principles. To his credit, he also vowed that an incident such as this, where a student's First Amendment rights were trampled upon by the college, would not happen again.

Society needs to take a strong stance against suppression of speech on campuses. Unfortunately, most people do not think of this issue until some egregious incident, like the one at Penn State, comes to the forefront. Many times, the harm will have already happened, but as in the law, an issue is not moot if it is capable of repetition. Considerable pressure will be placed on colleges and universities to police themselves in the coming years.

Part of this debate over academic freedom is going to include the awarding of permanent tenure to professors. Tenure is essentially a lifetime appointment, and it is a bone of contention to just about everyone except those who have it or aspire to it. The underlying rationale behind tenure is not job security; it is academic freedom. The ability of a professor to speak out without fear of losing his or her job is essential to the pursuit of vigorous debate. The political correctness movement that swept across campuses throughout the decade of the 1990s should be evidence enough of the need for tenure within academe. Even with it, some professors felt uneasy about voicing opposition to PC causes. Without it, debate would have shut down entirely because the politically expedient course for administrators was to embrace PC principles. How easy it would have been for administrators to shut down the opposition had tenure not been an obstacle.

Nevertheless, the tenure system at colleges and universities is under attack. People, including many inside academic circles, view tenure as protection for unproductive faculty members who contribute little to the academic environment. Undoubtedly, as we move into the next century, the tenure system on campuses will be overhauled. Although reform is not necessarily a bad thing, if the free speech principles embodied in tenure are not retained, the infringement of the First Amendment on campuses today will seem mild in comparison to what lies ahead.

SPEECH WE DON'T WANT TO HEAR

The booster shot given to talk radio this decade has also reminded us that we sometimes hear things we would rather not. People are understandably concerned about the culture of rage and hatred that has become so commonplace on our nation's airwaves. Beyond talk radio, politically charged, hateful messages are espoused and communicated by groups living on the fringe of society. Many Americans fear that the murderous words uttered by a paramilitary subculture cross over the line of protected speech. Still, no evidence has been produced that those who listen to these messages have carried out the despicable acts so often encouraged.

Accordingly, society needs to step back and reassess what the real danger is in allowing such speech to continue, whether in the back woods of a rural area or over the clear-channel signal of a metropolitan-area radio station. Many people today too quickly urge the silencing of the non-mainstream viewpoint. In support they cite the violent potential of the message, forgetting that incitement to violence is already an exception to general free speech principles. But the speaker must cross the line between advocating ideas and advocating action. The most frightening part of this notion is that people are so willing to use suppression as a tool to accomplish a laudable objective. This should sound familiar, for it is the same argument that can be brought in just about every First Amendment violation raised in these pages. Businesspeople say they file SLAPPs to silence troublemakers who interfere with their commercial enterprises. Academic administrators can say they are simply trying to create a nonhostile environment on campus when they sanction unpopular or distasteful remarks. Judges want to avoid another O. J. Simpson debacle, so they keep cameras out of their courtrooms. Politicians want to keep violent and sexual content out of motion pictures or television, so they pressure Hollywood and require a V-chip. Politicians want to ensure that children do not receive pornographic pictures over their computer screens, so they criminalize what would be protected in print. Juries want to punish the arrogant press with a whopping verdict. The list goes on. Unfortunately, so does the erosion of the First Amendment.

Taste also plays a critical role in the public's appetite for radio regulation. Howard Stern and Don Imus are constantly under attack by media watchdog groups for their sometimes off-color discourse. Both Stern and Imus are entertainers with huge followings. Their programs are broadcast in markets where plenty of alternative choices exist on the band. In other words, under a marketplace theory, if people do not wish to hear a particular program, they simply turn the dial.

Sadly, fewer and fewer people are getting agitated about the decline of free speech protection. Americans who support the result are also buying into the means suggested for accomplishing the goal. All of us need to recognize that we can support a result without endorsing the First Amendment-violative mechanism designed to arrive at it. The creative energy that once was the hallmark of American society is now too often replaced with unimaginative suppression of free speech for what could be called the greater good. The goals mentioned above can be achieved, but ingenuity must be rekindled. The greater good must once again encompass the liberty for which a revolution was fought.

Many Americans have lost sight of the real ingredients for freedom. During the tumultuous and divisive flag-burning debates in the early part of the 1990s, a constant refrain from proponents of restrictive statutes was that "soldiers had died for that flag." If anything dishonored fallen troops, it was that statement, heard time and again from politicians to pundits to habitués of corner taverns. Legions of American soldiers paid the ultimate price for the *liberties* that flag represents. Included among those liberties are the rights embodied in the First Amendment. Consequently, a circular argument passed for logic: Honor fallen soldiers by dissolving a freedom they fought to preserve. Once again, as is sadly so often the case, logic fell prey to emotion.

WHERE ARE WE GOING?

Technology helps shape us. Information technology plays a major role in shaping our society, and it always has. In the 1920s and 1930s, when entrepreneurs recognized the commercial viability of radio, they called on government for help in preserving the medium for the transmission of information and entertainment. Television continued to develop ways to distribute information with visual acumen. Cable found a way to diversify what viewers received, and the latest entree into the technological arena — the Internet — provides an interactive menu of instantaneous information.

The technology shares a common bond in terms of the First Amendment. All technologies that distribute information have faced challenges to free expression. Historical lessons should demonstrate that attempts by government to regulate information content conveyed by technology face strong constitutional challenges. But technology can be used to suppress. The V-chip, now to be included in all new television sets, in conjunction with a governmentally "requested" rating system, will take its toll on creative free expression.

The haste with which lawmakers are willing to bypass constitutional freedoms to aid a politically expedient cause célèbre should give all Americans pause. New technologies should be embraced and given the opportunity to grow and to help us grow as a society. Using regulations to stifle creativity and the full potential of these media is harmful not only to our constitutional safeguards but also to our citizens' ability to be full players in an exciting information society.

PRESCRIPTION FOR THE FIRST AMENDMENT

As with all living creatures, proper health care for the First Amendment — a living document — is crucial to its survival. Americans who recognize the need for protected expression often wonder what can be done to ensure the continued vitality of the First Amendment. The first step is education in its broadest sense, and this does not necessarily mean formal schooling. Reading about the First Amendment (presumably, readers of this section are about to complete such a task) is one sure way to gain the knowledge necessary to sustain a fight to keep the rights embodied in it. The second step is a willingness to fight for these rights, and sometimes a fight is necessary. Knowing when and whom to fight comes from a keen sense of understanding the issues in the world around us.

The operational definition of *world* is much smaller than it appears. Most infringements on speech, particularly ones that have a direct impact on people, occur at the local level. Citizens need look no further than their school boards, city and town councils, police departments, or state-operated entities to find violations of expressive freedoms. The buzzword is vigilance — a neighborhood watch of sorts —

over what is taking place in local communities. Vigilance carries with it a presumed duty to act. Waiting for the local media to locate the problem and work to correct it most times proves frustrating and fruitless. But the media will usually respond if prodded by the human interest element — that is, by the involvement of citizens. Human beings are a tremendous catalyst for protecting liberties.

If, for example, a school board removes certain books from the shelves of school libraries because its collective conservative ideology does not approve of the messages conveyed through the literature, citizens should act. Closing off young people's access to ideas is anathema to the First Amendment. The Internet will be a ripe area for school censorship. The media would likely report the board's action, but a major piece of the story is the people's response. One factor that media organizations use to gauge newsworthiness is the reaction the incident causes. Keeping watch over government is not always easy, and often that is by design of those in government.

Indeed, knowing when expressive freedom is in jeopardy is not always an easy task either, as has been demonstrated throughout this book. The efforts to restrict speech on behalf of local governments especially are wholly imaginative and difficult to spot. Take for example, a school board that restricts public commentary by holding its meetings in a very small room and filling the room with its administrators — making it extremely difficult for a citizen to make comments at or even attend board meetings. Is this restricting the citizens' rights to free expression and to petition the government?

Too often local government bodies refuse citizens access to information or to the board members themselves, knowing full well that the citizens will not likely wage a court battle for their rights — it would be too costly. Unfortunately, the boards sometimes do this on advice of legal counsel. Consider the irony of a solicitor, paid by public funds, advising a government body, also paid by the public, to restrict the rights of the public benefactor — a sad, and all too often, occurrence.

The adage that there is safety in numbers can be adapted to First Amendment battles as well. The one thing government officials typically pay attention to is a concerted effort on the part of vocal citizens to effect reform. A grassroots campaign for free speech can begin with a few phone calls to neighbors, and it can be greatly enhanced by an op-ed piece or a friendly editorial in the local newspaper. Open phones on call-in radio talk shows provide an excellent forum for making the public aware of a problem. In the SLAPP arena, for example, using the media to sharply denounce the oppressive tactics of business is often highly successful. Both businesses and government have a low tolerance for bad publicity.

In launching a First Amendment battle, citizens should try to locate a sympathetic news reporter. Such a relationship can yield benefits not only in terms of coverage but also in forming a connection to a powerful influence in the community — one with resources, such as a newspaper or a television station. Creating those same kinds of alliances with some friendly government officials is also useful. Often times, a lone voice on a board is willing to turn up the heat on colleagues if he or she is convinced of public backing.

In summary, the future of free expression rests with those whose liberty it broadly protects — all Americans. It is not too late, but waiting for someone else to carry freedom's torch — to stand up for expressive rights — will hasten the erosion of this cornerstone of democracy, the First Amendment.

Appendix: Select World Wide Web Sites

American Bar Association

The major trade association for attorneys. The site sets out the services of the association and general information on the profession.

Address: http: //www.abanet.org/

California Anti-SLAPP Project

Provides up-to-date information on the status of SLAPP suits nationwide. Links to other sites with SLAPP information are also available.

Address: http: //www.sirius.com/~casp/welcome. html

Center for Democracy and Technology

This site provides information on government attempts to regulate technology. A good source of information on the litigation around the Communications Decency Act.

Address: http: //www.cdt.org/

Electronic Frontier Foundation
Another source of information on technology and free speech in cyberspace.

Address: http: //www.eff.org/pub/Legal/

Federal Communications Commission
This government agency's site enables visitors to access information on regulations governing the communications industries.

Address: http: // lcweb.loc.gov/global/executive/fcc.html

Federal Communications Law Journal
Timely law review articles related to regulatory aspects of communications.

Address: http: / /www.law.indiana.edu/fclj /fclj.html

Federal Court Locator
Enables visitors to access judicial opinions from the federal circuits.

Address: http: //www.law.vill.edu/Fed-Ct/ fedcourt.html

Find Law
This site helps visitors locate sources of law.

Address: http: //www.findlaw.com.index.html

First Amendment CyberTribune
A site devoted to First Amendment in cyberspace issues. Contains links to other First Amendment sites.

Address: http: //w3.trib.com.FACT/

FOI Center
This is the site for the FOI Center at the University of Missouri. It contains useful resources on freedom of information issues.

Address: http: // www.missouri.edu/ ~foiwww/ index.html

Freedom Forum First Amendment Center
This web site of the Freedom Forum First Amendment Center in Nashville, Tennessee, contains a number of excellent resources on the First Amendment, including the center's monthly newsletter, devoted to First Amendment issues.

Address: http: //www.fac.org/

Government Printing Office
Enables visitors to retrieve government documents.

Address: http: //thorplus.lib.purdue.edu.gpo/

Legal Information Institute

This site contains several links to case locators and law school libraries.

Address: http: //www.law.cornell.edu/

Library of Congress

This direct link to one of the largest depositories of information in the world contains useful information and links to other federal government resources.

Address: http: //www.loc.gov/

National Archives

Another federal government treasure trove of information, including information on the founding documents of the nation.

Address: http: //www.nara.gov/

National Law Journal

The web site of a weekly publication of legal news.

Address: http: //www.ljextra.com/nlj/

Oral Argument Page

This site contains the audio recordings of the oral arguments of landmark United States Supreme Court cases.

Address: http: //oyez.at.nwu/oyez.html

Reporters Committee for Freedom of the Press

A site that is full of useful information and updates on media law, particularly as it pertains to journalism.

Address: http: //www.rcfp.org/rcfp/

Roll Call

The electronic edition of the newspaper of Capitol Hill.

Address: http: //www.rollcall.com/

Thomas

This is a government site enabling visitors to obtain copies and check the status of bills in Congress.

Address: http: //thomas.loc.gov/

United States House Law Library

Legal research resource material from the law library of the House of Representatives.

Address: http: //law.house.gov/

West's Legal News

Contains news and information from one of

the leading legal publishing companies in the United States.

Address: http: //www.westpub.comm/wlntop

Endnotes

CHAPTER TWO

1. *Frederick Post*, August 27, 1991, p. A1.
2. Ibid.
3. Letter from "Concerned Citizens of Frederick County," dated August 23, 1991, and incorporated as part of the record in *O'Brien v. Benna*, Case No. 3051L, Circuit Court for Frederick County, Maryland, June 23, 1992.
4. *Frederick Post*, August 30, 1991, p. A7.
5. Speech to the ALI-ABA Seminar on Strategic Lawsuits Against Public Participation, August 19, 1994, San Francisco, California.
6. 472 U.S. 479, 481 (1985).
7. Ibid., p. 483.
8. Ibid.
9. 376 U.S. 254 (1964). This case was the product of the country's mood during the heyday of the civil rights movement. The Court used the case as a vehicle for enhancing a citizen's right to fully participate in governmental affairs.

10. *McDonald*, 472 U.S. at 486. Note that "actual malice" is a legal term of art with a very specific definition, which should not be confused with the common understanding of malice — ill will, spite, or hatred. The actual malice requirement has been included in several states' responses to SLAPP and will be discussed later in this chapter.

11. *New York Times*, 376 U.S. at 279-80. In the opinion, Justice Brennan underscored "a profound national commitment to the principle that debate on public issues should be uninhibited, robust, and wide-open, and that it may well include vehement, caustic, and sometimes unpleasantly sharp attacks on government and public officials."

12. *Los Angeles Times*, October 4, 1991, p. A3.

13. Ruling of the Court, *O'Brien v. Benna*, Case No. 3051L, Circuit Court for Frederick County, Maryland, June 23, 1992.

14. *O'Brien v. Benna*, per curiam opinion, Case No. 1407, Court of Special Appeals of Maryland.

15. 573 N.Y.S.2d 105 (Misc. 1991).

16. Ibid., p. 109.

17. Penelope Canan and George W. Pring, "Studying Strategic Lawsuits Against Public Participation," 22 *Law & Society Review* 385 (1988).

18. 517 N.Y.S.2d 741 (A.D. 2d 1987).
19. Ibid.
20. Ibid., p. 742.
21. Ibid., p. 743.
22. Ibid., p. 744.
23. *Sherrard v. Hull*, 456 A.2d 59, 61 (Md. Ct. Spec. App. 1983).
24. Ibid.
25. 559 F. Supp. 1231, 1233 (D. Colo. 1983).
26. Ibid.
27. Ibid., p. 1236.
28. Ibid.
29. *Karnell v. Campbell*, 501 A.2d 1029, 1036 (N.J. Super. 1985).
30. Ibid.
31. S. 5441, New York Senate, 1991-1992 regular session.
32. Ibid., p. §70-a.
33. 376 U.S. 254 (1964). *See* New York S. 5441 §76-a (2).
34. New York S. 5441 §76-a (2).
35. California Code of Civil Procedure §425.16.
36. Washington Rev. Code §424.510.
37. Washington Rev. Code §4.94.185.
38. Florida House Bill 759; Senate Bill 2188 (1992) and House Bill 185; Senate Bill 70 (1993).
39. Jon L. Shebel, "A Perspective on SLAPP Suits in Florida," Associated Industries of Florida, 1993, p. 1.1.
40. Ibid., p. 1.4.

41. *Cape Cave Corporation v. Thomas W. Reese, et al.*, Case No. 85-1005CA, Summary Judgment, Circuit Court for Charlotte County, Florida, July 25, 1986.
42. Virginia Senate Bill 424 (1992).
43. New Jersey Senate Bill 3136 (1990).
44. Texas House Bill 149 (1990) and House Bill 7266 (1993).
45. Connecticut House Bill 1026; Senate Bill 182; Senate Bill 248; legislation introduced in 1991 as Raised Bill 7374 similarly failed.
46. Tennessee Senate Bill 52; House Bill 609 (1993).
47. Pennsylvania House Bill 281 (1995).
48. Westbrooke v. Miramar, Inc., Case No. 93-27502 (03), Permanent Injunction, Circuit Court, Broward County, Florida, November 16, 1993.
49. Patricia Walsh, "Homeowner, Developer Agree to Bury Hatchet," *Miami Herald*, November 19, 1993, Section BR, p. 1.
50. H. Harreld, "Tracking Coastal," *Triangle Business Journal*, vol. 11, no. 34, April 26, 1996, p. 1.
51. B. Hershberg, "Insurance Furor Stirs Lawsuits at Humana's Nevada Hospital," *Courier-Journal*, May 24, 1989, p. 16B.
52. P. Kenkel, "Reports of Overcharges, Suit Over Nevada Health Plan Weighing Humana Down," *Modern Healthcare*, June 8, 1992.
53. J. Nemes, "Humana to Ask Nevada Judge

to Overturn Award," *Modern Healthcare*, December 16, 1991, p. 3.

54. S. Whaley, "Measure Targets Lawsuits," *Las Vegas Review Journal*, February 27, 1997, p. 1B.

55. "Cancer Centers File Libel Suits Against MD Critics," *NCAHF Newsletter*, vol.15, no.6, p. 2.

56. Penelope Canan, Michael Hennessy, and George Pring, "The Chilling Effect of SLAPPs: Legal Risks and Attitudes Toward Political Involvement," 6 *Research in Political Sociology* 347 (1993).

CHAPTER THREE

1. 505 U.S. 377 (1992).

2. Mari J. Matsuda, "Public Response to Racist Speech: Considering the Victims' Story," 87 *Michigan Law Review* 2320, 2322 (1989).

3. Ibid., p. 2338.

4. Ibid., p. 2357.

5. Ibid., pp. 2364-65.

6. Rhonda G. Hartman, "Hateful Expression and First Amendment Values: Toward a Theory of Constitutional Constraint on Hate Speech at Colleges and Universities After *R.A.V. v. St. Paul*," 19 *Journal of College and University Law* 343, 357 (1993).

7. Ibid., p. 358.

8. Ibid., p. 359.

9. Nat Hentoff, *Free Speech for Me — But Not*

for Thee (New York: HarperPerennial, 1992), p. 153.

10. Ibid., p. 154.
11. Ibid., p. 155.
12. Chapter UWS 17.06.
13. *UWM Post v. Board of Regents of the University of Wisconsin System*, 774 F. Supp. 1163, 1167 (E.D. Wis. 1991).
14. Ibid., p. 1172.
15. *Doe v. University of Michigan*, 721 F. Supp. 852, 853 (E.D. Mich. 1989).
16. Ibid., p. 856.
17. Ibid., p. 853.
18. Ibid., p. 858.
19. Ibid., p. 867.
20. Ibid., p. 868, quoting *New York Times*, October 15, 1986, p. A27.
21. "Campus Speech Codes Are Being Shot Down as Opponents Pipe Up," *Wall Street Journal*, December 22, 1993, p. 1.
22. "Penn Explains Why It Did It," *Philadelphia Inquirer*, December 3, 1993, p. A27.
23. "Spanier's Free Expression Stance Supported," *Penn State Intercom*, vol. 26, no. 26, April 3, 1997, p. 2.
24. *Centre Daily Times*, April 24, 1993, p. 2B.
25. "Good Enough to Steal," *Student Press Law Center Report*, vol. XIV, no. 3, Fall 1993, p. 4.
26. *Student Press Law Center Report*, vol. XVII, no. 3, Fall 1996.

CHAPTER FOUR

1. "Summary of TV Cameras in the State Courts," National Center for State Courts, November 1, 1995.
2. "Facts and Opinions About Cameras in Courtrooms," a position paper by Court TV, July 1995, Appendix A.
3. Ibid., p. iii.
4. *Sheppard v. Maxwell*, 384 U.S. 333 (1966).
5. Cooper, Cynthia L. and Sam Reese Sheppard, *Mockery of Justice: The True Story of the Sheppard Murder Case* (Boston: Northeastern University Press, 1995), p. 16.
6. Ibid., pp. 64-65.
7. Ibid., p. 67.
8. 384 U.S. at 354.
9. *Sheppard v. Maxwell*, No. 65-490, Brief of Petitioner, p. 15 (1965).
10. Ibid., p. 22.
11. Ibid., p. 33.
12. Ibid., p. 38 (emphasis in the original).
13. 384 U.S. at 344.
14. Ibid., p. 356.
15. Ibid., pp. 358, 363.
16. Ibid., p. 363.
17. 381 U.S. 532, 595 (1965).
18. 449 U.S. 560 (1981).
19. Ibid., pp. 573-74.
20. The First Amendment guarantees that "Congress shall make no law . . . abridging freedom of the press. . . ." This clause has

been interpreted to mean that no governmental entity shall be permitted to interfere with the workings of a free press. Yet the interpretation has been subject to numerous exceptions. Consequently, it is often necessary to look to Supreme Court rulings for guidance on a particular issue.

21. *Richmond Newspapers v. Virginia,* 448 U.S. 555 (1980).
22. *Press-Enterprise v. Superior Court,* 464 U.S. 501 (1984).
23. *Press-Enterprise v. Superior Court,* 478 U.S. 1 (1986).
24. U.S. Const. amend. VI (1791).
25. "Facts and Opinions About Cameras in Courtrooms," a position paper by Court TV, July 1995, p. 7.
26. 448 U.S. 555, 572 (1980) [quoting *State v. Schmit,* 139 N.W.2d 800, 807 (1966)].
27. Ibid., p. 571.
28. Ibid., pp. 572-73.
29. Transcript of *This Week with David Brinkley,* June 26, 1994.
30. Ibid.
31. Ibid.
32. "Facts and Opinions About Cameras in Courtrooms," a position paper by Court TV, July 1995, p. 21.
33. Ibid., p. 14.
34. *Sharon Rufo, et al. n/a v. Orenthal James Simpson,* order dated August 23, 1996.

CHAPTER FIVE

1. 491 U.S. 397 (1989).
2. *Tinker v. Des Moines Independent Community School District,* 393 U.S. 503, 506 (1969).
3. Bethel School District No. 403 v. Fraser, 478 U.S. 675, 681 (1986).
4. Ibid., p. 691.
5. *Hazelwood v. Kuhlmeier,* 484 U.S. 260 (1988).
6. 395 U.S. 444 (1969).
7. The "clear and present danger test" was articulated by Justice Oliver W. Holmes in the 1919 case of *Schenck v. United States* (249 U.S. 47). Holmes wrote: "The question in every case is whether the words used are used in such circumstances and are of such a nature as to create a clear and present danger that they will bring about the substantive evils that Congress has a right to prevent."
8. 395 U.S. at 447.
9. "Will Pinkston, Profile: The G. Gordon Liddy Show, a.k.a. Radio Free D.C.," *The Fairness Forecast: Free Speech, Fair Play and Talk Radio,* the Freedom Forum First Amendment Center at Vanderbilt University, p. 26.
10. *Federal Radio Act of 1927,* 44 Stat. 1162 (1927).
11. See, e.g., "In the Matter of Editorializing by Broadcast Licensees," 13 F.C.C. 1246 (1949).

12. *Red Lion Broadcasting v. F.C.C.*, 395 U.S. 367, 375 (1969).
13. Ibid., p. 385.
14. See *Telecommunications Research & Action Ctr. v. F.C.C.*, 801 F.2d 501 (D.C. Cir. 1986) and *Meredith Corp. v. F.C.C.*, 809 F.2d 863 (D.C. Cir. 1987).
15. 45 *Cong. Q. Weekly Rep.* 3185 (1987).
16. *Spence v. Washington*, 418 U.S. 405 (1974).
17. Ibid., p. 412.
18. *Smith v. Goguen*, 415 U.S. 566, 574 (1974).
19. 491 U.S. 397 (1989).
20. Ibid., p. 403.
21. Ibid., pp. 407-408, quoting 337 U.S. 1, 4 (1949).
22. Ibid., p. 406.
23. Ibid., p. 422.
24. *United States v. Eichman*, 496 U.S. 310, 315 (1990).
25. "*Rice v. Paladin Enterprises, Inc.,*" 24 *Med. L. Rptr.* 2185 (1996).
26. Ibid., p. 2186.
27. D. Savage, "Appellate Judge Decries How-to Kill Book," *Los Angeles Times*, May 8, 1997, p. A20.
28. 24 *Med. L. Rptr.* at 2188.
29. Ibid., pp. 2191-92.
30. Ibid., p. 2193.
31. *First Amendment News*, vol. 2, no. 9, The Freedom Forum First Amendment Center, September 1996, p. 3.

32. *Los Angeles Times*, May 8, 1997, at A20.

33. *R.A.V. v. St. Paul*, 505 U.S. 377 (1992).

34. Ibid., p. 380, citing St. Paul, Minn., Legis. Code §292.02 (1990).

35. Ibid., p. 391.

36. *Wisconsin v. Mitchell*, 508 U.S. 476, 487 (1993).

37. 18 U.S.C. 248 (1996).

38. Robert Pear, "Abortion Clinic Workers Say Law Is Being Ignored," *New York Times*, September 23, 1994, p. A16.

39. *Madsen v. Women's Health Center*, 512 U.S. 753 (1994).

40. 67 F. 3d 359, 371 (2d Cir. 1994).

CHAPTER SIX

1. *The Telecommunications Act of 1996*, Public Law 104-104, §502 [directing the Federal Communications Commission to amend 47 U.S.C. section 223(a)].

2. Ibid. [directing the Federal Communications Commission to amend 47 U.S.C. section 223 (d)(1)].

3. Memorandum by Judge Ronald L. Buckwalter, *American Civil Liberties Union et al., v. Janet Reno*, U.S. District Court (E.D. Pa.), February 15, 1996.

4. Center for Democracy and Technology, Trial Bulletin No. 6, http://www.cdt.org., March 22, 1996.

5. Ibid.

6. Center for Democracy and Technology,

Trial Bulletin No. 9, http://www.cdt.org., April 13, 1996.

7. *ACLU et al. v. Reno*, Civil Action No. 96-963, and *American Library Association v. United States Department of Justice*, No. 96-1458 (E.D. Pa.), June 11, 1996.

8. Ibid.

9. Ibid.

10. *Reno, et al. v. ACLU, et al.*, No. 96-511, slip opinion.

11. Ibid.

12. Ibid., concurring opinion.

13. "Ohio Senate Abandons Amendment on Content Blocking Software," *Communications Today*, May 22, 1997.

14. H. Hartley, "Checking Out *Hustler* at the Library," *Chicago Tribune*, May 18, 1997, p. 22.

15. P. Baker, "Promoting Internet Links for All Students, Clinton Suggests 'V-Chip'-Type Limits," *Washington Post*, May 23, 1997, p. A13.

CHAPTER SEVEN

1. *Rosenblatt v. Baer*, 383 U.S. 75 (1966).

2. *Curtis Publishing Co. v. Butts*, 388 U.S. 130 (1967).

3. *Gertz v. Robert Welch, Inc.*, 418 U.S. 323 (1974).

4. *New York Times Co. v. Sullivan*, 376 U.S. 254, 270 (1964).

5. Ibid., pp. 279-80.

6. 390 U.S. 727, 731 (1968).
7. *Facts on File World News Digest*, April 18, 1996, p. 266 G1.
8. "Inquirer Settles Libel Suit with Sprague," *Pennsylvania Law Weekly*, April 8, 1996, p. 2.
9. Dan Biddle, "Above the Law," *Philadelphia Inquirer*, May 15, 1983, p. 1.
10. *McDermott v. Biddle*, 647 A.2d. 514, 526 (Pa. Super. 1994)
11. *McDermott v. Biddle*, 674 A.2d 665, 668 (Pa. 1996)
12. "$58 Million Awarded in Biggest Libel Verdict," *New York Times*, April 21, 1991, p. L19.
13. *Weller v. American Broadcasting Co., Inc.*, 19 *Med. L. Rptr.* 1161 (1991).
14. D. Tedford, "Judge to Hear Oral Argument in Libel Case Against Newspaper," *Houston Chronicle*, April 10, 1997, p. A22.
15. "Dow Jones Seeks to Upset $222.7 Million Libel Verdict," *Legal Intelligencer*, April 23, 1997, p. 4.
16. S. Borreson, "Libel Blitz," *Texas Lawyer*, March 31, 1997, p. 1.
17. Ibid.
18. Alabama, Arizona, Colorado, Florida, Georgia, Idaho, Louisiana, Mississippi, Ohio, Oklahoma, South Dakota, and Texas.
19. Robert D. Richards, "Truth in Vegetables," *Washington Post*, April 17, 1996, p. A23.

20. 418 U.S. at 339-40.
21. 497 U.S. 1 (1990).
22. Ibid., p. 5.
23. *Scott v. The News-Herald, et al.,* 496 N.E.2d 699, 708 (Ohio 1986).
24. See *Ollman v. Evans,* 750, 970 (D.C. Cir. 1984).
25. 497 U.S. at 18.
26. *Uniform Correction or Clarification of Defamation Act,* section 3.
27. Ibid., section 5.

CHAPTER EIGHT
1. "Artists, Accepting Federal Grants, Worry About Strings," *New York Times,* March 10, 1990, p. 117.
2. William H. Honan, "Head of Endowment for the Arts Is Forced From His Post by Bush," *New York Times,* February 22, 1992, p. A1.
3. 20 U.S.C. section 854 (d) (1).
4. *Findley v. National Endowment for the Arts,* 795 F. Supp. 1457 (C.D. Cal. 1992).
5. *Findley v. National Endowment for the Arts,* No. 92-56028, United States Court of Appeals (9th Circuit, November 5, 1996).
6. "The Arts Turn on the Star Power," *Washington Post,* March 12, 1997, p. D1.
7. D. Hudson, "Censoring of This Paint Way Out of Bounds," *Tennessean,* May 2, 1997, p. 9A.
8. " 'Gwen' Goes to Court," *First Amendment*

News, Freedom Forum First Amendment Center, vol. 3, no. 3, March 1997, p. 3.

9. C. Trevision, "Artist Finds Her Victory Bittersweet," *Tennessean*, April 30, 1997, p. 10D.

10. "Artistic Freedom Under Attack," *People for the American Way*, vol. 4, 1996.

11. Rock Out Censorship home page, http://www.ultranet.com/~crowleyn/ frspch.html.

12. Neil Strauss, "Wal-Mart CD Standards Are Changing Pop Music," *New York Times*, November 12, 1996, p. A1.

13. Ibid.

14. According to music censorship watchdog group Massachusetts Music Industry Coalition, the musicians currently targeted by this campaign are as follows: Wu-Tang Clan, Too Short, the Notorious B.I.G., Geto Boys, Tha Dogg Pound, Rappin' 4-Tay, 2 Pac Shakur, Gravediggaz, Onyx, Dove Shack, Bone Thugs-n-Harmony, MC Eiht, Cypress Hill, MC Ren, Cannibal Corpse, Ol' Dirty Bastard, Lords of Acid, Junior M.A.F.I.A., RBX, Black Crowes, and Blues Traveller.

15. Alan Bash, "New Code: Top Shows TV 14," *USA Today*, December 20-22, 1996, p. 1A.

16. T. Shales, "TV's Ratings: G Is for Give Them a Chance," *Washington Post*, March 9, 1997, p. G1.

CHAPTER NINE

1. 424 U.S. 1 (1976).
2. In its opinion in *Buckley v. Valeo*, the Supreme Court prefaced its treatment of the specific legislation at issue with a brief discussion of this general principle. To this end, the Court noted that "[t]he First Amendment affords the broadest protection to such political expression in order 'to assure [the] unfettered interchange of the ideas for the bringing about of political and social changes desired by the people.' Although First Amendment protections are not confined to 'the exposition of ideas,' there is practically universal agreement that a major purpose of that Amendment was to protect the free discussion of governmental affairs . . . of course includ[ing] discussion of candidates. . . . [citations omitted]."
3. 424 U.S. at 19.
4. Ibid., p. 18, footnote omitted.
5. Ibid., p. 19.
6. Ibid.
7. Ibid., p. 30. The Court cited its earlier opinion in *Williams v. Rhodes*, 393 U.S. 23, 32 (1968).
8. Ibid., p. 20.
9. Ibid., p. 21.
10. Ibid., p. 29.
11. *First Amendment News*, the Freedom Forum First Amendment Center, vol. 2, no. 12,

December 1996, p. 6.

12. Ibid.

13. G. McDonald, "Senate Rejects Campaign Reform Move," *Houston Chronicle*, March 19, 1997, p. A1.

14. NBC News transcript, *Meet the Press*, March 23, 1997.

15. www.publicampaign.org.

16. N. Ornstein, T. Mann, P. Taylor, M. Malbin, and A. Corrado, "Reforming Campaign Finance," issued by the Brookings Institute, December 17, 1996; revised May 7, 1997.

17. Ibid. The Brookings position paper includes detailed explanations on how these suggested reforms would work.

CHAPTER TEN

1. *Plessy v. Ferguson*, 163 U.S. 537 (1896).

2. 347 U.S. 483 (1954).

3. J. Sweeney, "Lungren Lashes Out at Glorification of Larry Flynt," *Copley News Service*, January 29, 1997.

4. *Hopwood, et al v. State of Texas*, 84 F.3d 720 (5th Cir. 1996).

Select Bibliography

Baker, C. Edwin. *Human Liberty and Freedom of Speech*. New York and Oxford: Oxford University Press, 1989.

University of Pennsylvania law professor C. Edwin Baker analyzes the "marketplace of ideas" concept in free speech and finds that it is not persuasive. Instead, he argues for the "liberty" theory.

Bollinger, Lee C. *Images of a Free Press*. Chicago: University of Chicago Press, 1994.

This book examines the relationship between law and journalism as developed through U.S. Supreme Court cases.

Bollinger, Lee C. *The Tolerant Society*. New York and Oxford: Oxford University Press, 1986.

Bollinger explores the accepted wisdom that society benefits from protecting "extremist" speech.

Bosmajian, Haig A. *Freedom of Expression*. New York: Neal-Schuman, 1987.

This book traces the tradition of silencing dissent in society.

Bracken, Harry M. *Freedom of Speech: Words Are Not Deeds*. Westport, Conn.: Praeger, 1994.
Bracken looks at the origin of the absolutist approach to free speech and traces its roots to the seventeenth-century proponents of religious tolerance.

Campbell, Douglas S. *Free Press v. Fair Trial: Supreme Court Decisions Since 1807*. Westport, Conn.: Praeger, 1994.
This book analyzes the conflict between a free press and the accused's right to a fair trial by looking at how the U.S. Supreme Court has reconciled the two positions over time.

Chafee, Zechariah Jr. *Free Speech in the United States*. Cambridge, Mass.: Harvard University Press, 1954.
This book is a landmark work from one of the principal First Amendment theorists of this century.

Cleary, Edward J. *Beyond the Burning Cross: The First Amendment and the Landmark R.A.V. Case*. New York: Random House, 1994.
The author examines the victory for the First Amendment in the U.S. Supreme Court's decision in *R.A.V. v. City of St. Paul*, a highly inflammatory cross-burning case.

de Grazia, Edward. *Girls Lean Back Everywhere: The Law of Obscenity and the Assault on Genius.* New York: Vintage Books, 1992.

This work traces the history of the obscenity problem in the United States and in Britain and offers some solutions.

Delfattore, Joan. *What Johnny Shouldn't Read: Textbook Censorship in America.* New Haven and London: Yale University Press, 1992.

Delfattore looks at textbook censorship in the United States from elementary through secondary schools.

Eldridge, Larry D. *A Distant Heritage: The Growth of Free Speech in Early America.* New York: New York University Press, 1994.

The author looked at more than 1,200 seditious speech prosecutions in colonial America and found that early Americans experienced a major expansion of their freedom to criticize the government.

Emerson, Thomas I. *The System of Freedom of Expression.* New York: Vintage Books, 1971.

One of the top First Amendment scholars sets out his theory of the First Amendment.

Fish, Stanley. *There's No Such Thing as Free Speech and It's a Good Thing, Too.* New York: Oxford University Press, 1994.

A Duke University scholar champions the

cause of the political correctness movement in America.

Freedman, Monroe H., and Eric M. Freedman. *Group Defamation and Freedom of Speech: The Relationship Between Language and Violence.* Westport, Conn.: Greenwood Publishing Group, Inc., 1994.
This book examines how defamation of groups can create an environment that encourages hatred and oppression.

Freedman, Warren. *Freedom of Speech on Private Property.* New York; Westport, Conn.; and London: Quorum Books, 1988.
Freedman attempts to answer the question of how First Amendment protection can be extended to both public and private property.

Garry, Patrick. *Scrambling for Protection: The New Media and the First Amendment.* Pittsburgh: University of Pittsburgh Press, 1994.
The author looks at the application of First Amendment principles to new communications technologies and how current law will have to change to handle new media.

Haiman, Franklyn S. *"Speech Acts" and the First Amendment.* Carbondale and Edwardsville, Ill.: Southern Illinois University Press, 1993.
Haiman examines the distinction between symbolic and nonsymbolic transactions and how

speech and action have been treated under the First Amendment.

Hentoff, Nat. *Free Speech for Me — But Not for Thee.* New York: Harper Collins, 1992.
  Hentoff argues that censorship is the "strongest drive in human nature."

Ingelhart, Louis E. *Press Law and Press Freedom for High School Publications.* New York; Westport, Conn.; and London: Greenwood Press, 1986.
  This work looks at what First Amendment protections are available to the student press.

Kalven, Harry Jr. *A Worthy Tradition: Freedom of Speech in America.* New York, Philadelphia, San Francisco, Washington, and London: Harper and Row, 1988.
  A comprehensive examination of U.S. Supreme Court decision making in the First Amendment area.

Lane, Robert W. *Beyond the Schoolhouse Gate: Free Speech and the Inculcation of Values.* Philadelphia: Temple University Press, 1995.
  Lane traces free expression in public schools beginning with *Tinker v. Des Moines Independent Community School District* in 1969 to the present.

Lewis, Anthony. *Make No Law: The Sullivan*

Case and the First Amendment. New York: Random House, 1991.

This veteran legal writer looks at the impact of the landmark U.S. Supreme Court case on defamation law and free speech generally.

McWhirter, Darien A. *Exploring the Constitution Series: Freedom of Speech, Press, and Assembly.* Phoenix, Ariz.: Oryx Press, 1994.

In this part of a series on the Constitution, McWhirter looks at the evolution of the free speech doctrine in this country.

Pally, Marcia. *Sex & Sensibility: Reflections of Forbidden Mirrors and the Will to Censor.* Hopewell, N.J.: Ecco Press, 1994.

Pally provides an academic look at the rush to censorship in America.

Pring, George W., and Penelope Canan. *SLAPPs: Getting Sued for Speaking Out.* Philadelphia: Temple University Press, 1996.

A study of Strategic Lawsuits Against Public Participation (SLAPPs) from the inventors of the term.

Rose, Lance. *Netlaw: Your Rights in the Online World.* Berkeley, New York, and London: McGraw-Hill, 1995.

Rose has developed a guidebook to rights in the on-line frontier, including free speech, privacy, and adult materials.

Shiffrin, Steven H. *The First Amendment, Democracy, and Romance.* Cambridge, Mass., and London: Harvard University Press, 1990.

Professor Shiffrin argues that Ralph Waldo Emerson and Walt Whitman might have more to teach us about the First Amendment and democracy than do the more notable First Amendment scholars.

Smith, Craig R., editor. *The Diversity Principle: Friend or Foe of the First Amendment.* Washington, D.C.: The Media Institute, 1989.

This work explores how the notion of diversity has been misapplied in some cases involving the media.

Smolla, Rodney A. *Free Speech in an Open Society.* New York: Alfred A. Knopf, 1992.

A thoughful reflection on the value of free expression in American society.

Smolla, Rodney A. *Jerry Falwell v. Larry Flynt: The First Amendment on Trial.* New York: St. Martin's Press, 1988.

Smolla looks at the controversial First Amendment case involving the publisher of *Hustler* magazine from the perspective of an "observer of the American scene."

Thaler, Paul. *The Watchful Eye: American Justice in the Age of the Television Trial.* Westport, Conn.: Praeger, 1994.

Thaler traces the history of the televised trial and its impact on American jurisprudence.

Van Alstyne, William W., editor. *Freedom and Tenure in the Academy*. Durham, N.C., and London: Duke University Press, 1993.
This Duke University law scholar has put together a collection of essays relating how academic freedom is intertwined with the concept of tenure at American colleges and universities.

Wagman, Robert J. *The First Amendment Book*. New York: Pharos Books, 1991.
A retrospective on free speech and free press, published for the two-hundredth anniversary of the First Amendment.

Walker, Samuel. *Hate Speech: The History of an American Controversy*. Lincoln, Neb.: University of Nebraska Press, 1994.
The author traces the evolution of hate speech in America, including group libel and its impact on the First Amendment.

About the Author

Robert D. Richards is an associate professor of journalism and law and the founding director of the Pennsylvania Center for the First Amendment at Pennsylvania State University. He is the author of *Uninhibited, Robust, and Wide Open: Mr. Justice Brennan's Legacy to the First Amendment* and a contributing author to *Mass Communications Law in Pennsylvania*. He has written numerous articles on the First Amendment for both the academic and the popular press. A former broadcast journalist, talk show host, and lawyer, Richards is a frequent commentator on First Amendment issues in the national media.